THE ULTIMATE CONGESTIVE HEART FAILURE COOKBOOK

150 Easy Recipes for Wellness & Longevity.

Sienna Currey

Table of contens

4

Foreword by Sienna Currey

Welcome to a journey of heart health, flavor, and transformation. My name is Sienna Currey, and I'm thrilled to share with you " The Ultimate Congestive Heart Failure Cookbook: 150 Easy Recipes for Wellness & Longevity." This book is more than just a collection of recipes; it's a reflection of my personal voyage through the challenges of living with Congestive Heart Failure (CHF) and my determination to turn a diagnosis into an opportunity for growth and health.

Like many of you, my journey wasn't easy. Being diagnosed with CHF was a wake-up call that prompted me to reevaluate my lifestyle, particularly my diet. I was faced with a daunting challenge: to navigate the complexities of a heart-healthy diet without sacrificing the joy of eating. It was a journey that took me from confusion and frustration to discovery and passion.

Armed with a desire to overcome my health obstacles, I embarked on a deep dive into the world of heart-healthy foods. I learned about the impact of sodium and fats on heart health and the importance of nutrient-rich ingredients. Along the way, I discovered that a diet designed to manage CHF doesn't have to be bland or restrictive. Instead, it can be a doorway to a world of innovative, delicious, and nourishing meals.

This book is the culmination of years of research, cooking, and firsthand experience. It's designed for individuals with CHF, their caregivers, and anyone interested in embracing a heart-healthy lifestyle. The recipes you'll find here are crafted with love, care, and a deep understanding of the dietary needs of those managing heart disease. But more than that, they are designed to delight the palate, nourish the body, and bring joy to the table.

Each recipe is a testament to the belief that food can be both healing and delicious. From energizing breakfasts and revitalizing lunches to satisfying dinners and delightful desserts, these meals are tailored to support heart health without compromising on taste. They are my gift to you, born from a journey that has transformed my life and, I hope, will positively impact yours.

As you turn the pages and explore these recipes, remember that every meal is an opportunity to nurture your heart and celebrate your health. I invite you to join me on this delicious adventure of culinary discovery and heart health. Together, let's take control of our heart health today and embrace a future of wellness and longevity.

Here's to our health, happiness, and the healing power of food.

Warmest regards,

Sienna Currey

.

Introduction

Heart health: two words that encapsulate a vast, essential aspect of our well-being, often taken for granted until warning signs or symptoms demand our attention. The heart, a symbol of life and emotion, plays a foundational role in our physical health, pumping life-giving blood to every cell in our bodies. This chapter begins our journey into understanding the heart—not just as an organ, but as the center of our vitality and a key to longevity.

Let me share a story that brings this home. A few years ago, a close friend of mine, Alex, experienced what he initially brushed off as stress and minor chest discomfort. He led a busy life, with little time spared for health check-ups or reflection on his well-being. It wasn't until a frightening episode of breathlessness forced him to the emergency room that he faced the reality of his heart's condition: early-stage congestive heart failure (CHF). This was a wake-up call not just for Alex but for all of us around him. It underscored a truth we often forget—taking care of our heart is not just about avoiding illness; it's about nurturing our life's essence.

Through Alex's journey, and now through this guide, we aim to illuminate the path to heart health. We start by understanding the heart itself and then move into the complexities of CHF, armed with knowledge, compassion, and a proactive stance towards health.

The Journey to Heart Health: Understanding Your Heart

The Heart Explained

Anatomy of the Heart

The heart, merely the size of a fist, is an engineering marvel situated in the chest cavity, slightly to the left. It comprises four chambers: the two upper atria and the two lower ventricles. These chambers work in a meticulously coordinated manner to pump blood throughout the body, delivering oxygen and nutrients to cells and removing waste products.

The right side of the heart receives oxygen-poor blood from the body and pumps it to the lungs, where it receives oxygen. The left side, meanwhile, receives this oxygen-rich blood from the lungs and pumps it throughout the body. This dual-role functionality underscores the heart's pivotal position in maintaining life, regulating everything from physical activity to the serene moments of rest.

How the Heart Works

Understanding how the heart works requires a glimpse into its daily, never-ending workload. With each beat, the heart contracts and relaxes, a cycle that propels blood through a vast network of blood vessels stretching nearly 60,000 miles. This cycle is regulated by electrical signals that ensure the heart beats at the right pace, adapting to our body's changing needs from moment to moment.

The heart's role extends beyond mere mechanics. It's integral in maintaining blood pressure, controlling blood supply based on the body's demands, and playing a critical part in the body's overall balance and homeostasis. Recognizing the heart's workload and complexity inspires awe and a renewed commitment to caring for this tireless organ.

Understanding Congestive Heart Failure (CHF)

What is CHF?

Congestive Heart Failure, often referred to simply as heart failure, is a condition where the heart's ability to pump blood effectively is compromised. It doesn't mean the heart has stopped working, but its efficiency in meeting the body's needs for blood and oxygen is reduced. CHF can affect either the left side, right side, or both sides of the heart, and it often develops gradually over time.

Causes and Risk Factors

The journey to CHF can begin through various pathways, each intertwining with aspects of lifestyle, health conditions, and sometimes, genetics. Common causes include coronary artery disease, high blood pressure, and diabetes, which over time can weaken or stiffen the heart, diminishing its ability to function effectively. Risk factors also encompass lifestyle choices such as smoking, obesity, and a sedentary lifestyle, alongside age and family history.

Understanding these causes and risk factors is crucial. It empowers us to make informed choices about our health, recognizing the power of prevention and the importance of managing existing health conditions with diligence and care.

Signs and Symptoms

The signs of CHF can be subtle at first, easy to dismiss as the effects of aging or a busy life. Breathlessness, persistent coughing or wheezing, swelling in the legs, ankles and feet, fatigue, and an increased heart rate are among the signals our bodies send us, indicating the heart is struggling.

Recognizing these symptoms early can be life-saving, prompting necessary changes in lifestyle and medical intervention. If you or someone you know experiences these symptoms, it's critical to seek medical advice. Early detection and management of CHF can significantly improve quality of life and outcomes, turning a potentially daunting diagnosis into a manageable condition.

Through understanding the heart and the intricacies of conditions like CHF, we embark on a path of proactive health management. This journey is not just about avoiding disease; it's about embracing a life of vitality, where heart health is a priority nurtured through informed choices, compassion, and a commitment to well-being.

Why Your Diet Matters: The Link Between Nutrition and Heart Function

The adage "You are what you eat" resonates profoundly when it comes to heart health. The intricate relationship between diet and the cardiovascular system is undeniable, with every morsel of food we consume acting either as a boon or bane to our heart's well-being. This connection is rooted in the way nutrients from our diet interact with the body's metabolic processes, influencing everything from blood pressure to cholesterol levels.

A heart-healthy diet can fortify the heart's defenses, reducing the risk of heart disease and improving the quality of life for those managing conditions like congestive heart failure (CHF). Conversely, diets high in unhealthy fats, excessive salt, and sugars can accelerate the path to heart disease, leading to a myriad of complications that compromise the heart's function and overall health.

Understanding this link is pivotal, guiding us towards dietary choices that nurture rather than neglect our heart. It empowers us to consciously embrace foods that support heart function, ultimately shaping our health destiny with each meal.

Nutrients and the Heart

The journey towards heart health is paved with a spectrum of nutrients, each playing a unique role in supporting the cardiovascular system. Here's an overview of key nutrients that are allies of heart health:

- **Omega-3 Fatty Acids:** Found in fatty fish like salmon, chia seeds, and walnuts, omega-3s are champions of heart health. They help reduce inflammation, lower blood pressure, and decrease triglyceride levels, offering a shield against heart disease.

- **Fiber:** A diet rich in fiber from fruits, vegetables, and whole grains can help improve cholesterol levels, reduce blood pressure, and promote overall heart health. Fiber aids in digestion and helps in maintaining a healthy weight, directly impacting heart disease risk.

- **Antioxidants:** Vitamins C and E, selenium, and flavonoids, found abundantly in fruits, vegetables, nuts, and seeds, act as the body's defense against oxidative stress, which can lead to heart disease over time.

- **Potassium:** This essential mineral helps regulate blood pressure by counteracting the effects of sodium. Foods like bananas, potatoes, and spinach are excellent sources.

- **Magnesium:** Involved in over 300 biochemical reactions in the body, magnesium supports heart rhythm and helps control blood pressure. Leafy greens, whole grains, and nuts are good sources.

Incorporating a variety of these nutrients into your diet can significantly impact heart health, offering protection and resilience against heart disease.

The Risk of Poor Diet Choices

While the path to heart health is laden with nutrient-rich foods that support vitality, the consequences of poor dietary choices loom large. Diets high in saturated and trans fats, excessive sodium, and added sugars pose significant risks to heart health. These unhealthy eating habits can lead to the accumulation of plaque in the arteries, high blood pressure, and increased risk of heart attacks and strokes.

- **Saturated and Trans Fats:** Found in fried foods, processed meats, and baked goods, can raise harmful cholesterol levels, contributing to arterial blockage.

- **Excessive Salt Intake:** Can cause the body to retain fluid, increasing blood pressure and the heart's workload.

- **Added Sugars:** Often hidden in processed foods and beverages, can lead to obesity and insulin resistance, both of which are risk factors for heart disease.

Recognizing these risks is not about fostering fear but about cultivating awareness and making informed choices. By understanding the detrimental impact of unhealthy eating habits, we can take proactive steps towards a diet that celebrates and supports heart health, paving the way for a life of wellness and longevity.

Embracing a heart-healthy diet is a journey of discovery, filled with the richness of natural flavors and the joys of nourishing your body and heart. As we continue to explore the power of dietary choices in managing heart health, remember that each step forward is a step towards a healthier heart and a more vibrant life.

Decoding Heart Healthy Diets: Beyond Low Sodium and Low Fat

For decades, heart health advice seemed straightforward: limit your salt and cut the fat. Yet, as our understanding of nutrition and cardiovascular disease deepens, it's clear this advice only scratches the surface. A genuinely heart-healthy diet is about balance, diversity, and the quality of the nutrients we consume. It's about moving beyond the binary of low sodium and low fat to embrace a more holistic view of what it means to eat for heart health.

Understanding Nutritional Balance

The Myth of Low Fat: The early dietary guidelines prescribing low-fat diets overlooked the complexity of fats and their role in our health. Not all fats are created equal, and healthy fats, such as those from avocados, nuts, and fish, are crucial for heart health. They help manage cholesterol, reduce inflammation, and provide essential fatty acids that our bodies cannot produce on their own.

The Role of Sodium: While excessive sodium intake can lead to high blood pressure, a risk factor for heart disease, sodium itself is not the enemy. It's a vital mineral essential for nerve function, muscle contractions, and fluid balance. The key is moderation and choosing natural sources of sodium over processed foods, which often contain high levels.

A Spectrum of Nutrients: A heart-healthy diet encompasses a wide range of nutrients, including vitamins, minerals, fiber, and antioxidants. These nutrients support heart function, reduce inflammation, and help prevent arterial damage. Incorporating a variety of foods into your diet ensures you receive these essential nutrients in the right balance.

Key Components of a Heart-Healthy Diet

- **Fruits and Vegetables:** The foundation of any heart-healthy diet, fruits, and vegetables, are rich in fiber, vitamins, and antioxidants. They're linked to lower rates of heart disease and can help manage blood pressure and reduce the risk of stroke.

- **Whole Grains:** Replacing refined grains with whole grains can improve heart health. Whole grains contain more fiber, which helps lower cholesterol and makes you feel full, aiding in weight management.

- **Lean Proteins:** Sources of lean protein, including poultry, fish, legumes, and nuts, support muscle health without the added burden of saturated fats found in red meat.

- **Healthy Fats:** Emphasizing unsaturated fats found in olive oil, nuts, and fatty fish can help improve cholesterol levels and offer anti-inflammatory benefits.

Dietary Patterns for Heart Health

- **Mediterranean Diet:** Rich in fruits, vegetables, whole grains, olive oil, and fish, the Mediterranean diet has been shown to reduce the risk of heart disease significantly.

- **DASH Diet:** Specifically designed to combat high blood pressure, the Dietary Approaches to Stop Hypertension (DASH) diet emphasizes fruits, vegetables, whole grains, and lean proteins while limiting salt, sugar, and saturated fats.

- **Plant-Based Diets:** Eating patterns that focus on plant-based foods are associated with lower risks of heart disease. These diets are high in fiber, vitamins, and phytonutrients that support heart health.

Challenges and Considerations

- **Reading Food Labels:** Understanding food labels is crucial for making heart-healthy choices. Learn to identify key nutrients and watch out for hidden sources of sodium and saturated fats.

- **Portion Control:** Managing portion sizes helps control caloric intake and maintain a healthy weight, reducing the strain on your heart.

- **Mindful Eating:** Paying attention to what and how you eat can improve your dietary choices and lead to better heart health. Mindful eating encourages a more connected and enjoyable eating experience, focusing on the quality rather than the quantity of food.

Practical Tips for Adopting Heart-Healthy Eating Habits

- **Meal Planning:** Planning meals can help ensure you include a variety of heart-healthy foods in your diet. Consider preparing meals in advance to control ingredients, portions, and nutritional balance.

- **Cooking Techniques:** Opt for cooking methods that preserve the nutritional value of food and reduce unhealthy additives. Grilling, baking, and steaming are excellent choices.

- **Eating Out:** Making heart-healthy choices when dining out can be challenging. Look for menu items that are grilled, baked, or steamed, and don't hesitate to request modifications to fit your dietary needs.

Decoding heart-healthy diets reveals that optimal nutrition for cardiovascular health extends well beyond reducing sodium and fat intake. It's about embracing a diverse, balanced diet rich in whole foods that support heart function and overall well-being. By understanding the components of a heart-healthy diet and adopting dietary patterns that emphasize nutritional quality, we can take significant strides toward improving our heart health and living a longer, more vibrant life.

Chapter 1: Building Your Heart-Healthy Pantry: Essential Ingredients for Everyday Cooking

Welcome to the first step on your journey toward a heart-healthy lifestyle. "Building Your Heart-Healthy Pantry: Essential Ingredients for Everyday Cooking" is more than just a chapter; it's a blueprint for transforming your kitchen—and by extension, your health. The path to managing congestive heart failure and preventing heart disease begins with what we put on our plates, and that starts with what we stock in our pantries.

A heart-healthy diet doesn't have to be restrictive or bland. On the contrary, it can be an exploration of flavors, textures, and nutrients that not only nourish the heart but also delight the senses. The key lies in selecting ingredients that are low in sodium and unhealthy fats, rich in fiber, and packed with the vitamins and minerals essential for cardiovascular health. This chapter will guide you through each category of pantry essentials, explaining why they're beneficial and how they fit into a heart-healthy diet.

We'll delve into the world of whole grains, legumes, nuts, seeds, herbs, spices, healthy oils, fruits, vegetables, and lean proteins, offering practical advice on selecting, storing, and incorporating these ingredients into your daily meals. Additionally, we'll provide shopping tips to help you navigate the grocery store aisles, making heart-healthy choices that are both budget-friendly and delicious.

Organizing your pantry with heart health in mind sets the stage for nutritious meal preparation and helps reinforce healthy eating habits. By the end of this chapter, you'll have the knowledge and tools to build a pantry that supports your heart health goals, making it easier to cook and enjoy meals that are not only good for your heart but also good for your soul.

Embrace this journey with an open heart and a willingness to explore the rich diversity of heart-healthy foods. Your pantry is the heart of your kitchen; let's ensure it reflects your commitment to a healthier, happier heart.

Understanding Heart-Healthy Ingredients

Embarking on a journey to heart health through nutrition requires a fundamental understanding of what makes certain ingredients beneficial for the heart. Heart-healthy ingredients are the cornerstone of a diet that aims to nourish and protect this vital organ. This section will explore the characteristics that define heart-healthy ingredients and delve into the pivotal role these nutrients play in maintaining cardiovascular health.

Defining Heart-Healthy Ingredients

Heart-healthy ingredients can be defined by several key characteristics: they are low in sodium, low in saturated and trans fats, high in dietary fiber, and rich in essential nutrients. Each of these attributes plays a crucial role in supporting heart health, contributing to a balanced diet that can help manage and prevent heart disease.

- **Low in Sodium:** Sodium is a mineral essential for bodily functions, including fluid balance and muscle function. However, excessive sodium intake is linked to high blood pressure, a significant risk factor for heart disease. Heart-healthy ingredients are low in sodium, helping to maintain normal blood pressure levels and reduce the strain on the heart.

- **Low in Saturated and Trans Fats:** Saturated fats, found in animal products and some plant oils, can raise LDL (bad) cholesterol levels in the blood, increasing the risk of heart disease. Trans fats, often found in processed foods, are even more harmful, raising LDL cholesterol while also lowering HDL (good) cholesterol. Ingredients low in these fats contribute to a healthier lipid profile, reducing the risk of plaque buildup in the arteries.

- **High in Dietary Fiber:** Dietary fiber is a plant-based nutrient that the body cannot digest. Soluble fiber, in particular, can help lower blood cholesterol levels by binding to cholesterol in the digestive system and removing it from the body. High-fiber ingredients can also improve satiety, aiding in weight management—a key factor in heart health.

- **Rich in Essential Nutrients:** Heart-healthy ingredients are abundant in vitamins, minerals, and antioxidants that support cardiovascular health. These include potassium, which can help counteract the effects of sodium and lower blood pressure; magnesium, which is involved in over 300 biochemical reactions in the body, including those that regulate heart rhythm and blood pressure; and antioxidants, which protect the body against oxidative stress and inflammation, both of which can contribute to heart disease.

The Role of These Nutrients in Heart Health

The nutrients found in heart-healthy ingredients play a multifaceted role in supporting cardiovascular health and preventing heart disease. Understanding this role provides a clearer picture of why these ingredients are essential in a heart-healthy diet.

- **Managing Blood Pressure:** High blood pressure, or hypertension, is a major risk factor for heart disease. Ingredients low in sodium and rich in potassium and magnesium help regulate blood pressure levels. Potassium, for example, helps balance the amount of sodium in the body, while magnesium helps relax the blood vessels, both of which can lower blood pressure.

- **Improving Cholesterol Levels:** Maintaining healthy cholesterol levels is crucial for heart health. Ingredients high in soluble fiber, such as oats and legumes, can reduce the absorption of cholesterol into the bloodstream. Moreover, replacing saturated and trans fats with unsaturated fats, found in ingredients like avocados, nuts, and olive oil, can improve the lipid profile by lowering LDL cholesterol and increasing HDL cholesterol.

- **Reducing Inflammation:** Chronic inflammation is a key player in the development of heart disease. Antioxidant-rich ingredients, such as berries, leafy greens, and whole grains, can help neutralize free radicals and reduce inflammation, protecting the heart and blood vessels from damage.

- **Weight Management:** Obesity is a significant risk factor for heart disease. Ingredients high in dietary fiber are more filling, which can help control appetite and aid in weight management. Healthy weight management reduces the burden on the heart and decreases the risk of developing heart disease.

Incorporating Heart-Healthy Ingredients into Your Diet

Understanding what defines heart-healthy ingredients and their role in cardiovascular health is the first step toward incorporating these foods into your daily diet. By choosing ingredients that are low in sodium and unhealthy fats, high in fiber, and rich in essential nutrients, you can craft meals that are not only delicious but also deeply nourishing for your heart.

As we move forward in this chapter, we will explore specific heart-healthy pantry staples, providing practical advice on selecting, storing, and utilizing these ingredients in everyday cooking. The goal is to make heart-healthy eating a sustainable, enjoyable part of your lifestyle, leading to lasting benefits for your heart health and overall well-being.

Heart health is not just about avoiding certain foods; it's about embracing a diet that celebrates and utilizes the vast array of nutritious, flavorful ingredients that nature provides. With each heart-healthy choice, you're taking a step toward a healthier heart and a more vibrant life.

The Heart-Healthy Pantry Essentials

Crafting a detailed exploration of the essentials for a heart-healthy pantry is not just about listing beneficial foods; it's about understanding how each ingredient contributes to cardiovascular health and how to seamlessly integrate them into your daily meals for a nourishing, balanced diet. This section will delve into the key pantry staples that form the foundation of heart-healthy cooking, providing practical insights and inspiration for their use.

Whole Grains

Transitioning from refined grains to whole grains is a fundamental step towards a heart-healthy diet. Whole grains retain all parts of the grain, including the fiber-rich bran and nutrient-packed germ, offering a complete package of health benefits. They are instrumental in regulating blood pressure and improving heart health due to their high fiber content, which also aids in maintaining healthy cholesterol levels. Examples of whole grains to stock in your pantry include quinoa, known for its complete protein profile; brown rice, which boasts a rich mineral content; and whole wheat pasta, offering a fiber-filled alternative to its refined counterpart. Integrating whole grains into your diet can be as simple as swapping white rice for farro or bulgur, adding a nutrient-dense twist to familiar meals.

Legumes

Beans and lentils are powerhouses of nutrition, offering a hearty dose of fiber, protein, and essential minerals like iron and potassium. Their high fiber content not only supports digestive health but also plays a role in cholesterol management, contributing to cardiovascular well-being. Legumes are versatile and economical, making them an ideal component of a heart-healthy pantry. Incorporating them into your diet can range from adding chickpeas to salads for a protein boost to using lentils as a base for flavorful stews and soups.

Nuts and Seeds

Nuts and seeds are excellent sources of healthy fats, protein, and fiber, contributing to heart health by lowering LDL (bad) cholesterol and improving arterial health. Almonds, walnuts, and flaxseeds, for example, are rich in omega-3 fatty acids, known for their anti-inflammatory properties and ability to prevent heart disease. Including a small handful of nuts as a snack or sprinkling seeds over salads or yogurt can easily increase your intake of these nutritious fats. However, moderation is key due to their high-calorie content.

Herbs and Spices

Herbs and spices are invaluable for adding flavor without the need for excess salt, a crucial consideration for maintaining heart health. Options like garlic powder, turmeric, cinnamon, and rosemary not only enhance taste but also offer various health benefits, including anti-inflammatory and antioxidant properties. Experimenting with different herbs and spices can elevate the taste of dishes while supporting your heart health goals.

Healthy Oils

Choosing the right oils for cooking and dressing is critical for heart health. Olive oil, particularly extra-virgin olive oil, stands out for its content of monounsaturated fats and polyphenols, which support heart health by reducing inflammation and protecting against oxidative stress. Avocado and walnut oils are also excellent choices, offering similar benefits. These oils can replace saturated fats in the diet, contributing to a healthier heart.

Fruits and Vegetables

A colorful array of fruits and vegetables should be the cornerstone of a heart-healthy diet. Packed with antioxidants, vitamins, and fiber, they fight inflammation, support healthy blood pressure, and reduce the risk of heart disease. Each color represents different nutrients, so aiming for a variety of hues ensures a broad spectrum of health benefits. Whether fresh, frozen, or canned (with no added salt or sugar), incorporating fruits and vegetables into every meal is a delicious and easy way to support heart health.

Lean Proteins

Protein is essential for maintaining muscle health and overall bodily functions, but the source of protein is crucial for heart health. Lean protein sources, including poultry without the skin, fish, especially fatty fish rich in omega-3 fatty acids like salmon and mackerel, and plant-based options like tofu and tempeh, provide the necessary nutrients without the added saturated fats. Integrating these proteins into your diet supports heart health by promoting healthy cholesterol levels and reducing the risk of heart disease.

Incorporating Heart-Healthy Essentials into Your Diet

Creating a heart-healthy pantry is about more than just stocking up on nutritious foods; it's about learning to incorporate these essentials into your daily cooking in ways that are both delicious and beneficial for your heart. From starting the day with oatmeal topped with walnuts and berries to enjoying a quinoa salad with mixed vegetables for lunch, the possibilities are endless. The key is creativity and variety, ensuring that your meals are not only good for your heart but also pleasing to your palate.

By understanding the role of each of these pantry staples in promoting heart health and learning to incorporate them into your meals, you're taking significant steps toward a diet that supports not just your heart, but your overall well-being. Remember, a heart-healthy diet is a journey, one that involves making informed choices about the foods you eat and enjoying the myriad of flavors and textures they bring to your table.

Shopping Tips for a Heart-Healthy Pantry

Navigating the grocery store with the goal of stocking a heart-healthy pantry requires a strategic approach. This section will delve into practical shopping tips that ensure you fill your cart with ingredients beneficial for heart health, without straining your budget. Understanding how to read labels, choose between fresh and processed options, and shop economically can make maintaining a heart-healthy diet an achievable goal.

Reading Labels for Hidden Sodium and Fats

One of the first skills to master in shopping for heart-healthy ingredients is label reading. Food labels provide essential information about the nutritional content of items, but they can also hide the truth about sodium and fat content behind confusing terms or serving sizes.

- **Sodium:** Look beyond the "low sodium" claim by checking the milligrams of sodium per serving. Remember, the American Heart Association recommends no more than 2,300 milligrams a day, moving toward an ideal limit of 1,500 milligrams per day for most adults. Be wary of terms like "sodium-free," "reduced sodium," and "no salt added," as these can still contain sodium.

- **Fats:** While scanning for fats, differentiate between the types of fats listed. Saturated and trans fats are the ones to avoid or limit for heart health. Seek products with higher amounts of monounsaturated or polyunsaturated fats instead. Beware of the term "partially hydrogenated oils," a significant source of trans fats.

- **Serving Sizes:** Pay attention to the serving size and the number of servings per container. Sometimes, what seems like a single serving is actually more, skewing the perception of how much sodium and fat you're consuming.

Choosing Fresh Versus Canned or Processed Foods

Incorporating more fresh ingredients into your diet is a cornerstone of heart-healthy eating. However, canned or processed foods can sometimes be a convenient and affordable alternative, provided you make informed choices.

- **Fresh Foods:** Fresh fruits, vegetables, and lean meats are ideal for a heart-healthy diet. They contain the highest levels of nutrients and the least amount of unhealthy additives. Shopping seasonally and locally can also enhance flavor and nutritional content while supporting your community.

- **Canned Foods:** When choosing canned goods, opt for low-sodium or no-salt-added versions. For canned fruits, look for those packed in water or their own juice, avoiding syrups. Always drain and rinse canned foods to reduce sodium content further.

- **Processed Foods:** While it's best to limit processed foods, not all are off-limits. Read labels carefully to choose healthier options. Look for whole-grain bread and pasta, and check for added sugars, sodium, and saturated fats in packaged meals.

Budget-Friendly Shopping for Heart-Healthy Ingredients

Eating heart-healthy doesn't have to break the bank. With some planning and smart shopping strategies, you can enjoy nutritious meals without overspending.

- **Bulk Purchases:** Buying whole grains, legumes, nuts, and seeds in bulk can save money in the long run. Store them properly to extend their shelf life.

- **Seasonal Produce:** Fresh fruits and vegetables are often more affordable when in season. Plus, they're at their peak of flavor and nutrition. Consider freezing extra portions for off-season use.

- **Sales and Coupons:** Keep an eye on sales and use coupons for heart-healthy products. Many stores also offer discounts on certain days of the week or month.

- **Plan Your Meals:** Meal planning can reduce impulse buys and ensure you purchase only what you need. Make a list based on weekly meals and stick to it.

- **Store Brands:** Often, store-brand products are similar in quality to name brands but are less expensive. Compare labels to ensure you're getting a heart-healthy option.

- **Limit Junk Food:** Not only is junk food bad for your heart, but it also adds unnecessary costs to your grocery bill. Focus your budget on nutrient-dense foods that contribute to your health.

Equipping yourself with the knowledge and skills to shop for heart-healthy ingredients is a significant step towards a nutritious diet that supports cardiovascular health. By learning to read labels carefully, making informed choices between fresh and processed foods, and adopting budget-friendly shopping strategies, you can build a pantry that not only supports heart health but also fits your lifestyle and budget. Remember, every food choice is an opportunity to nourish your heart and embrace a healthier future.

Organizing Your Pantry for Heart Health

Organizing your pantry is akin to laying the groundwork for a heart-healthy diet. A well-structured pantry not only makes it easier to select nutritious ingredients for every meal but also inspires and facilitates healthier eating habits. This section provides comprehensive guidance on organizing your pantry in a way that prioritizes heart health, ensuring that healthier choices are always within reach and less healthy temptations are minimized.

Embracing Pantry Organization for Heart Health

- **Start with a Clean Slate:** Begin by emptying your pantry. This initial step allows you to take stock of what you have, discard expired items, and identify less healthy options that can be replaced with heart-healthier alternatives.

- **Categorize for Convenience:** Group items by category, such as whole grains, legumes, nuts and seeds, canned goods, spices, and oils. This not only makes it easier to find what you need but also helps in meal planning around heart-healthy ingredients.

- **Prioritize Accessibility:** Place heart-healthy staples at eye level or within easy reach. This subtle nudge can make a significant difference in daily food choices, naturally gravitating you and your family towards healthier options.

- **Use Clear Containers:** Store whole grains, legumes, and seeds in clear, airtight containers with labels. This practice not only prolongs shelf life but also allows you to see what you have at a glance, making it more likely that you'll use these nutritious ingredients.

- **Dedicate Space for Heart-Healthy Snacking:** Create a section in your pantry for heart-healthy snacks like unsalted nuts, seeds, and dried fruits (with no added sugars). Having these snacks readily accessible can curb the temptation for less healthy options.

Gradually Replacing Less Healthy Options

- **Phase Out Processed Foods:** Identify processed foods that are high in sodium, saturated fats, and added sugars. Gradually reduce their presence in your pantry by not restocking them once they run out. Instead, replace them with whole, minimally processed alternatives.

- **Switch to Whole Grains:** If your pantry is stocked with refined grains like white rice, pasta, and bread, start by introducing their whole-grain counterparts. You don't have to make the switch all at once. Begin by mixing whole grains with refined ones until your palate and recipes are fully adjusted to the healthier option.

- **Upgrade Your Oils:** Evaluate the oils in your pantry. Gradually replace hydrogenated oils and those high in saturated fats (like coconut oil) with heart-healthy oils such as olive oil, avocado oil, and flaxseed oil.

- **Rethink Your Cans:** Canned goods can be a convenient pantry staple but often come loaded with sodium. Gradually replace them with low-sodium or no-salt-added versions, and consider increasing your stock of fresh or frozen fruits and vegetables.

- **Introduce More Legumes:** If legumes are not already a staple in your pantry, start by adding one or two varieties, such as black beans or lentils. They can serve as a base for numerous heart-healthy dishes, from salads to stews.

- **Herbs and Spices Over Salt:** Reduce your reliance on salt by expanding your collection of herbs and spices. As you explore more flavors, you'll find you can achieve delicious results in your cooking without the need for excess sodium.

Making Heart-Healthy Pantry Organization a Habit

- **Regular Check-ins:** Make it a habit to periodically review your pantry's contents. This regular audit helps ensure that heart-healthy staples remain at the forefront of your cooking habits and that less healthy items don't creep back in.

- **Involve the Family:** Pantry organization can be a family affair. Involving family members in the process can help everyone become more aware of heart-healthy eating habits and contribute to meal planning and preparation.

- **Stay Informed:** As nutritional science evolves, so too might the definition of what's considered heart-healthy. Stay informed about the latest dietary guidelines and research to ensure your pantry reflects the most current health advice.

- **Celebrate Diversity:** A heart-healthy pantry is also a diverse pantry. Regularly introducing new whole grains, legumes, nuts, seeds, and spices can keep meals exciting and encourage a broader intake of essential nutrients.

Organizing your pantry with heart health in mind is an empowering step towards a sustainable, nutritious diet. By making heart-healthy ingredients the easiest and most appealing choices, you lay a foundation for meals that not only nourish the heart but also satisfy the palate. This organized approach to stocking and using your pantry also facilitates a gradual transition away from less healthy options, making the journey towards heart health a positive and enjoyable experience.

Embracing this organizational strategy does more than just simplify meal prep; it transforms your pantry into a treasure trove of ingredients that support your heart's health. With every meal crafted from this well-organized space, you're not just feeding your family; you're loving their hearts.

Practical Application

Transitioning to a heart-healthy diet is not just about knowing which foods to choose; it's also about learning how to incorporate these foods into your daily meals in a way that's both satisfying and delicious. This section, "Practical Application," aims to guide you through the process of utilizing your heart-healthy pantry staples in everyday cooking, making it easier to enjoy nutritious meals that benefit your heart.

Integrating Heart-Healthy Staples into Daily Meals

- **Morning Boost with Whole Grains and Seeds:** Start your day with a nourishing breakfast that leverages the power of whole grains and seeds. Prepare overnight oats using rolled oats, chia seeds, and almond milk. Top with fresh berries and a dollop of natural peanut butter for an added dose of antioxidants and healthy fats. Whole grains like oats are rich in soluble fiber, which can help lower cholesterol levels, while chia seeds add omega-3 fatty acids beneficial for heart health.

- **Legume-Based Lunches:** Legumes are versatile and can be the star ingredient of hearty, nutritious lunches. For a simple yet satisfying meal, toss cooked quinoa with black beans, diced tomatoes, avocado, and cilantro for a quinoa bean salad. Dress with lime juice and extra-virgin olive oil for a zesty flavor. This combination offers a great mix of protein, fiber, and healthy fats, making it perfect for supporting heart health.

- **Nuts and Seeds as Snack Options:** For snacks, rely on nuts and seeds to satisfy hunger and provide a nutrient boost. Mix unsalted almonds, walnuts, and pumpkin seeds for a homemade trail mix. Nuts and seeds are excellent sources of monounsaturated fats and omega-3 fatty acids, which are known to reduce inflammation and improve heart health.

- **Diverse Dinners with Lean Proteins and Vegetables:** Make lean proteins and a variety of vegetables the centerpiece of your dinner. Grill salmon fillets, seasoned with herbs like dill and served alongside roasted Brussels sprouts and sweet potatoes. Salmon is an excellent source of omega-3 fatty acids, while Brussels sprouts and sweet potatoes offer fiber, vitamins, and minerals essential for heart health.

- **Fruit-Based Desserts:** Cap off your day with a dessert that's both heart-healthy and satisfying. A simple fruit salad with mixed berries, sliced kiwi, and a sprinkle of chia seeds can satisfy your sweet tooth while providing antioxidants, vitamins, and fiber.

Incorporating heart-healthy ingredients into your daily cooking doesn't have to be complicated or time-consuming. By keeping your pantry stocked with the essentials and employing simple, flavorful combinations, you can enjoy meals that are not only delicious but also supportive of your cardiovascular health. The key is to experiment with these staples, finding ways to integrate them into your meals that align with your tastes and lifestyle. With each heart-healthy meal, you're taking a step towards a healthier heart and a more vibrant life.

Chapter 2: Planning for Success: Meal Planning and Prep Strategies for Everyday Cooking

Welcome to Chapter 2, "Planning for Success: Meal Planning and Prep Strategies." The journey to a heart-healthy lifestyle is paved with good intentions, but without a concrete plan, it can be challenging to navigate. This chapter is designed to transform your intentions into actions by equipping you with the knowledge and skills needed to plan and prepare meals that nourish your heart and delight your palate.

Embarking on this journey requires more than just knowing which foods to eat and which to avoid; it demands a thoughtful approach to how we organize, prepare, and think about our meals. For those managing congestive heart failure or looking to prevent heart disease, the stakes are even higher. The foods we choose play a critical role in controlling sodium and fat intake, maintaining balanced nutrition, and ultimately supporting heart function.

In this chapter, we delve into the fundamentals of meal planning tailored to the needs of heart health. We start by laying out the nutritional groundwork necessary for understanding the components of a heart-healthy diet. From there, we'll guide you through setting up a meal planning process that fits your lifestyle, utilizing tools and techniques that make planning efficient and effective.

Meal prep is more than a buzzword; it's a strategy that can significantly impact your ability to stick to a heart-healthy diet, especially when time is scarce. We'll explore practical tips for batch cooking, ingredient prep, and recipe modification, ensuring that you're never caught off guard without a nutritious meal option at hand.

But life is unpredictable, and flexibility is key. We'll discuss how to adapt your meal plans to accommodate changes in schedule, dietary needs, and even the preferences of family members, making heart-healthy eating a shared and enjoyable experience.

Through practical application, sample meal plans, and a step-by-step prep day blueprint, this chapter aims to set you on a path to success. Meal planning and preparation, when approached with knowledge and foresight, can become powerful tools in managing heart health, allowing you to take control of your diet and, by extension, your well-being. Let's embark on this journey together, one meal at a time.

The Basics of Heart-Healthy Meal Planning

Embarking on the path to a heart-healthy lifestyle through meal planning requires a foundational understanding of the dietary needs specific to heart disease and congestive heart failure. This section, "The Basics of Heart-Healthy Meal Planning," aims to equip you with the knowledge necessary to navigate these needs, guiding you towards making informed decisions that support heart health. Through understanding your dietary requirements and learning how to create a balanced plate, you can begin to see meal planning not just as a dietary restriction, but as a delicious opportunity for nurturing your heart.

Understanding Your Dietary Needs

- **Nutritional Requirements for Managing Heart Disease and Congestive Heart Failure:** The nutritional landscape for managing heart disease and congestive heart failure is vast, yet certain key principles emerge as universally beneficial. At its core, the diet aims to minimize the workload on the heart, reduce blood pressure, lower cholesterol levels, and prevent fluid retention. Achieving these goals involves a nuanced understanding of your body's needs, which include:

  - Low Sodium Intake: Aiming for no more than 1,500 to 2,300 milligrams of sodium per day is generally recommended.

  - Reduced Saturated and Trans Fats: Opting for lean proteins and substituting saturated fats with healthier fats can help manage cholesterol levels.

- High Fiber Foods: Incorporating a variety of fruits, vegetables, and whole grains into your diet can increase your fiber intake.

- Adequate Fluid Intake: Consulting with a healthcare provider to determine the right amount of fluid intake is crucial.

- Moderation in Alcohol and Caffeine: Limiting or avoiding alcohol and caffeine can be beneficial, especially for those with heart disease or heart failure.

Creating a Balanced Plate

- **Guidelines for Balancing Meals with the Right Proportions:** Here's how to structure a heart-healthy plate:

  - Fruits and Vegetables: Half of your plate should consist of fruits and vegetables.

  - Whole Grains: At least one quarter of your plate should be dedicated to whole grains.

  - Lean Proteins: The remaining quarter of your plate should include lean protein sources.

  - Healthy Fats: Incorporate healthy fats into your meals through cooking oils, dressings, and toppings.

Incorporating Heart-Healthy Foods into Every Meal

- **Breakfast:** Oatmeal topped with fresh berries and a sprinkle of chia seeds.

- **Lunch:** Salad with mixed greens, chickpeas or grilled chicken, and a vinaigrette made from olive oil and lemon juice.

- **Dinner:** Grilled salmon or a bean-based stew alongside quinoa and steamed vegetables.

- **Snacks:** Carrot sticks with hummus, a small handful of unsalted nuts, or a piece of fruit.

Understanding your dietary needs and knowing how to balance your plate are fundamental steps in heart-healthy meal planning. By focusing on low sodium, low saturated and trans fats, high fiber, and adequate fluid intake, you can create meals that support your heart health. Additionally, learning the art of balancing fruits, vegetables, whole grains, lean proteins, and healthy fats on your plate ensures that every meal brings you closer to your heart health goals. Meal planning, with this knowledge at its core, becomes an empowering tool in managing heart disease and congestive heart failure, paving the way for a healthier lifestyle.

Organizing Your Meal Planning Process

In the quest for heart health, especially when navigating the complexities of managing heart disease and congestive heart failure, organizing your meal planning process becomes not just a strategy for eating well but a cornerstone of daily self-care. This section, "Organizing Your Meal Planning Process," is dedicated to transforming meal planning from a daunting task into a streamlined, enjoyable part of your routine. By understanding your dietary needs, setting realistic goals, and utilizing modern tools and resources, you can create a meal planning system that supports your heart health and fits seamlessly into your life.

Understanding Your Dietary Needs

Before diving into meal planning, it's crucial to have a clear understanding of your unique dietary needs. This foundation ensures that the meals you plan not only contribute to your overall heart health but also address specific requirements and restrictions you may have, whether it's limiting sodium to manage blood pressure or balancing fluid intake for heart failure. Recognizing these needs will guide your meal selection, ingredient choices, and preparation methods, making each meal a step toward better heart health.

Setting Realistic Goals

- **Aligning with Lifestyle and Health Needs:** Meal planning should enhance your life, not become a source of stress. Start by setting achievable goals that reflect your lifestyle, daily routine, and health objectives. If you're new to meal planning, begin with planning just a few days at a time rather than an entire week. Consider your schedule: Are there days when cooking is simply not feasible? Plan for simpler meals or healthy leftovers for these times.

- **Gradual Implementation:** Incorporate heart-healthy changes gradually. If your current diet is far from the ideal heart-healthy diet, abrupt changes can feel overwhelming and unsustainable. Introduce one or two new recipes each week to slowly adjust your palate and preferences.

- **Flexibility Is Key:** While consistency in meal planning is beneficial, rigidity can lead to frustration. Life is unpredictable—unexpected events, changes in appetite, or even shifts in mood can affect your meal plan. Design your plan with flexibility in mind, allowing for easy swaps and last-minute changes without sacrificing nutritional value.

Meal Planning Tools and Resources

- **Leveraging Technology:** In the digital age, an array of tools and apps can simplify the meal planning process. Apps like Mealime and Eat This Much offer customizable meal plans that can cater to specific dietary needs, including low sodium or low fat, and generate shopping lists based on your plan. These tools can save time, reduce waste, and ensure variety in your diet.

- **Utilizing Templates and Printables:** For those who prefer something tangible, meal planning templates and printables available online can be invaluable. A well-designed template allows you to visualize your week, track your nutritional goals, and ensure a balanced diet. Find a template that includes sections for breakfast, lunch, dinner, and snacks to cover all bases.

- **Building a Recipe Collection:** Create a digital folder or a physical binder to collect and organize recipes that meet your heart-healthy criteria. This collection becomes a personalized resource that can inspire and guide your meal planning. Include notes on recipes you've tried, modifications you've made, and family feedback to refine your collection over time.

Organizing your meal planning process is a journey that begins with understanding your specific dietary needs and setting realistic, flexible goals. By incorporating modern tools, resources, and the support of a community, you can create a meal planning routine that not only supports your heart health but also enhances your quality of life. This organized approach to meal planning empowers you to make informed, intentional choices about your nutrition, laying a solid foundation for a heart-healthy lifestyle that is both fulfilling and sustainable. Remember, the goal of meal planning is not perfection but progress toward a healthier, happier heart.

Meal Prep Strategies for Busy Lives

In the realm of heart-healthy living, particularly for those navigating the challenges of heart disease or congestive heart failure, meal prep emerges not just as a convenience but as a critical component of dietary management. This section, "Meal Prep Strategies for Busy Lives," delves into practical approaches to meal preparation that accommodate the fast-paced nature of modern life while adhering to the dietary needs essential for heart health.

Understanding Your Dietary Needs

Before embarking on any meal prep journey, it's imperative to have a clear understanding of your specific dietary requirements. This insight ensures that the meals you prepare in advance align with your heart health goals, whether that involves managing sodium intake, controlling portions, or ensuring a balanced intake of nutrients. Tailoring your meal prep strategy to meet these needs can significantly enhance its effectiveness and ensure that your heart health remains a priority, even during the busiest of weeks.

Batch Cooking

Maximizing Efficiency with Bulk Preparation:

Batch cooking, the practice of preparing larger quantities of food at once, is a cornerstone of efficient meal prep. This approach not only saves time but also ensures that you have heart-healthy meals ready when time is scarce. When batch cooking, consider recipes that freeze well, such as soups, stews, and casseroles, making sure they align with your low sodium and low fat dietary goals. Utilize lean proteins, whole grains, and an abundance of vegetables to ensure these meals are both nourishing and satisfying.

Safe Storage and Reheating:

Proper storage is crucial to maintaining the safety and quality of your batch-cooked meals. Divide meals into portion-controlled containers that are freezer-safe and microwave-safe to facilitate easy reheating. Labeling containers with the contents and date of preparation can help keep track of what you have on hand and ensure that meals are consumed within an appropriate timeframe, generally within three months for frozen meals.

Efficient Use of Ingredients

Strategic Ingredient Selection:

Selecting ingredients that can be used across multiple meals throughout the week is a key strategy for minimizing waste and streamlining your meal prep process. Versatile ingredients like quinoa, lean chicken breast, and mixed vegetables can serve as the base for various dishes, from salads to stir-fries to soups. Plan your meals with these ingredients in mind, ensuring that you're making the most of the groceries you buy.

Creative Repurposing of Leftovers:

Transforming leftovers into new meals is an art that can add variety to your weekly menu while ensuring nothing goes to waste. Leftover roasted vegetables can be incorporated into whole-grain wraps, mixed into quinoa salads, or blended into a heart-healthy soup. Grilled chicken can be sliced into salads, added to whole-wheat pasta dishes, or used as a topping for homemade pizza on a whole-grain crust.

Prepping Ingredients Ahead

Streamlining the Cooking Process:

Dedicating time to prepping ingredients at the beginning of the week can significantly reduce the time required to assemble meals on busy nights. Washing, chopping, and portioning out vegetables, fruits, and lean proteins can make the process of putting together a nutritious meal much quicker and more efficient. Consider marinating proteins in heart-healthy marinades made with olive oil, lemon juice, and a variety of herbs and spices to enhance their flavor and tenderize them before cooking.

Organizational Techniques:

Utilizing clear, labeled containers for prepped ingredients can keep your refrigerator organized and make it easy to see what you have ready to use. This visual organization not only helps with meal assembly but also encourages the use of these healthy ingredients before they spoil. Implementing a first-in, first-out system ensures that older ingredients are used up first, minimizing waste and maximizing the freshness of your meals.

Embracing Flexibility in Meal Prep:

While prepping ingredients ahead is a time-saving strategy, it's important to maintain flexibility. Life can be unpredictable, and appetites can vary. Prepping ingredients instead of full meals provides the freedom to adjust your meal plan as needed, ensuring that your heart-healthy diet can adapt to your changing schedule and preferences.

Meal prep for busy lives, especially when tailored to the dietary needs of those managing heart disease or congestive heart failure, is a balancing act of preparation, efficiency, and flexibility. By embracing batch cooking, making efficient use of ingredients, and prepping components ahead of time, you can ensure that maintaining a heart-healthy diet doesn't fall by the wayside during hectic weeks. These strategies not only simplify the process of eating well but also reinforce the commitment to nurturing your heart health with every meal you prepare. Through thoughtful planning and a bit of creativity, meal prep can transform from a weekly chore into a key pillar of your heart-healthy lifestyle.

Adapting Meal Plans for Individual Needs

In the landscape of meal planning, especially within the context of heart health, the ability to tailor meal plans to fit individual dietary needs, preferences, and unexpected life events is paramount. This section, "Adapting Meal Plans for Individual Needs," delves into the nuances of personalizing your meal strategy. It encompasses understanding your unique dietary requirements, modifying recipes to meet specific health conditions or preferences, maintaining flexibility in the face of life's unpredictabilities, and engaging family members in the meal planning process to ensure it's inclusive and supportive of everyone's health and tastes.

Understanding Your Dietary Needs

At the heart of effective meal planning is a deep understanding of your personal dietary needs. This encompasses more than just knowing which foods to avoid or include; it's about recognizing how different nutrients interact with your body, particularly if you're managing conditions like heart disease or congestive heart failure. For instance, if you're on a low-sodium diet to manage blood pressure, understanding how to identify hidden sources of sodium in foods becomes crucial. Similarly, if you're aiming to lower cholesterol, knowledge about the types of fats and their effects on your lipid profile is essential. Begin by consulting with a healthcare provider or a dietitian to gain clarity on your dietary needs and how best to meet them through your meal plans.

Modifying Recipes

Tailoring Recipes to Your Diet:

Modifying recipes to align with your heart-healthy dietary goals doesn't mean sacrificing flavor or satisfaction. It involves creative substitutions and adjustments that ensure your meals are nutritious, enjoyable, and supportive of your health. For instance, swapping out salt for a blend of herbs and spices can dramatically reduce sodium intake while enhancing flavor. Using pureed avocado or unsweetened applesauce in place of butter in baked goods can lower saturated fat content and add heart-healthy fats or fiber. Whole wheat flour can replace white flour to increase the fiber content of your recipes.

Innovating with Ingredients:

Experimentation is key when adjusting recipes. Don't hesitate to replace ingredients that don't meet your dietary needs with those that do. For example, if a recipe calls for cream, consider using blended cashews or low-fat Greek yogurt as a substitute. Such innovations not only make recipes healthier but can also introduce you to new textures and flavors, enriching your culinary experience.

Flexibility in Meal Planning

Anticipating Changes:

Life is inherently unpredictable, and your meal plan should have the flexibility to accommodate last-minute changes. Create a "backup" list of quick, heart-healthy meals that can be prepared with pantry staples for days when time or resources are limited. Embrace the concept of "planned-overs" – intentionally preparing extra portions of meals that can be easily repurposed or enjoyed later in the week.

Adjusting on the Fly:

Developing the skill to adjust your meal plan on the fly, based on what's available or necessary due to dietary restrictions, is invaluable. This might mean swapping out one type of leafy green for another in your salad or using an alternative grain if your first choice is unavailable. Keeping a well-stocked pantry of versatile, heart-healthy ingredients can significantly aid in this flexibility.

Involving Family in Meal Planning

Shared Responsibility and Decision-Making:

Meal planning becomes more enriching and less burdensome when it's a shared family responsibility. Engage family members in the process by having each person suggest meals for the week. This not only ensures that everyone's tastes and dietary needs are considered but also fosters a sense of inclusion and teamwork.

Educational Opportunities:

Use meal planning as an opportunity to educate family members about heart health and nutrition. Explaining why certain foods are chosen or avoided can be an eye-opening experience for all, potentially inspiring healthier eating habits across the board. Encourage family members, including children, to read labels, understand nutritional content, and recognize the importance of heart-healthy eating.

Customization for Individual Needs:

In families where multiple dietary needs exist, customization becomes key. This might involve preparing a base meal that can be easily modified to suit individual preferences or dietary restrictions. For instance, a basic stir-fry can be adapted with different proteins or served over various grains to meet the needs of each family member. Encourage open dialogue about food preferences and health requirements to ensure meal plans are inclusive and supportive of everyone's health journey.

Adapting meal plans for individual needs is a dynamic, multifaceted process that plays a critical role in the success of heart-healthy eating. By understanding personal dietary requirements, modifying recipes to fit these needs, maintaining flexibility, and involving family in meal planning, you create a supportive, inclusive, and adaptable meal planning strategy. This approach not only ensures that your heart health is prioritized but also makes mealtime an opportunity for connection, education, and enjoyment. Embrace the flexibility and creativity this process brings, and let it guide you and your loved ones toward a lifestyle that supports heart health and overall well-being.

Practical Application and Examples

Embarking on a journey to enhance heart health through diet necessitates not just understanding but also applying principles of heart-healthy eating in practical, tangible ways. This section, "Practical Application and Examples," bridges the gap between theory and practice, providing a one-week sample meal plan tailored to the needs of individuals with congestive heart failure, focusing on low sodium, low fat, and nutrient-rich foods. Additionally, we offer a comprehensive prep day blueprint to streamline your meal preparation process, ensuring you can maintain this heart-healthy eating pattern even during your busiest weeks.

Understanding Your Dietary Needs

Recognizing the dietary needs specific to managing congestive heart failure is the cornerstone of effective meal planning. This means prioritizing foods that are naturally low in sodium and saturated fats, rich in fiber, and packed with antioxidants and essential nutrients. Such a diet aids in managing blood pressure, reducing the risk of heart complications, and promoting overall cardiovascular health.

Sample Meal Plan

- **Day 1:**
    - Breakfast: Oatmeal topped with fresh berries and a sprinkle of chia seeds.
    - Lunch: Grilled chicken salad with mixed greens, avocado, cucumber, and a vinaigrette dressing.
    - Dinner: Baked salmon with roasted Brussels sprouts and quinoa.

- **Day 2:**
  - Breakfast: Greek yogurt with sliced bananas and a drizzle of honey.
  - Lunch: Whole grain wrap with turkey breast, spinach, and mustard, served with carrot sticks.
  - Dinner: Stir-fried tofu with broccoli, bell peppers, and brown rice.

- **Day 3:**
  - Breakfast: Smoothie made with spinach, almond milk, banana, and a tablespoon of almond butter.
  - Lunch: Lentil soup with a side of whole-grain bread.
  - Dinner: Grilled shrimp over a mixed greens salad with a lemon-olive oil dressing.

- **Day 4:**
  - Breakfast: Scrambled eggs with diced tomatoes, spinach, and whole-wheat toast.
  - Lunch: Quinoa bowl with black beans, corn, diced tomatoes, and avocado.
  - Dinner: Baked chicken breast with steamed green beans and sweet potato.

- **Day 5:**
  - Breakfast: Overnight oats with almond milk, mixed nuts, and apple slices.
  - Lunch: Tuna salad (made with low-fat mayo) on whole-grain bread, served with sliced cucumber.
  - Dinner: Vegetable stir-fry with tofu and a side of brown rice.

- **Day 6:**
  - Breakfast: Whole grain pancakes topped with fresh fruit and a small amount of maple syrup.
  - Lunch: Chickpea and vegetable curry served over basmati rice.
  - Dinner: Turkey meatballs with whole-wheat spaghetti and a side salad.

- **Day 7:**
  - Breakfast: Fruit salad with a dollop of low-fat Greek yogurt and a sprinkle of flaxseed.
  - Lunch: Roasted vegetable and hummus wrap, served with an apple.
  - Dinner: Grilled lean steak with roasted asparagus and mashed cauliflower.

Prep Day Blueprint

1. **Shopping List Compilation:** Begin by making a detailed shopping list based on the meal plan. Organize your list by food categories (produce, protein, dairy, etc.) to streamline your shopping experience. Remember to check your pantry and refrigerator first to avoid purchasing items you already have.

2. **Ingredient Preparation:**
   - Wash and chop all vegetables needed for the week's meals. Store them in labeled containers in the refrigerator.

- Cook a large batch of quinoa and brown rice to use as sides or salad bases.

- Marinate proteins (chicken, tofu, fish) according to the recipes planned for the week. Store in the refrigerator if using within 2 days or freeze for later use.

- Pre-portion snacks like nuts, seeds, and chopped vegetables for easy access.

3. **Batch Cooking:**

- Prepare soups, stews, or casseroles that can be easily reheated throughout the week. Portion and freeze any meals you won't eat within the next few days.

- Bake or grill several portions of protein to be used in salads, wraps, or main dishes.

4. **Organizing Your Refrigerator and Pantry:**

- Allocate specific areas of your refrigerator for meal components – one shelf for proteins, another for prepped vegetables, and a drawer for fresh fruits.

- Use clear containers for all prepped ingredients and label them with contents and prep date to ensure freshness and ease of use.

5. **Flexible Meal Assembly:**

- For meals not fully pre-cooked, organize ingredients together in the refrigerator or pantry. For example, group all ingredients needed for a specific salad or stir-fry together, so you can quickly assemble the meal on the day it's planned.

Storage Tips:

- Ensure all containers are airtight to maintain freshness.

- Cool down cooked foods before refrigerating to prevent moisture build-up and spoilage.

- Use freezer-safe containers for meals that will be frozen, leaving enough space for food to expand.

Implementing a heart-healthy meal plan is an empowering step toward managing congestive heart failure and promoting overall cardiovascular health. This sample meal plan and prep day blueprint are designed to provide a solid foundation, from which you can adapt and personalize your approach to fit your dietary needs, lifestyle, and preferences. By dedicating time to plan and prepare your meals, you're investing in your heart health and well-being, ensuring that every meal brings

Chapter 3: Recipes for a Rejuvenated Heart

Energizing Breakfasts: Kickstart Your Day the Heart-Healthy Way

1. Sunrise Oat Berry Parfait

Yield: 2 servings | **Prep time:** 10 minutes | **Cook time:** 0 minutes

Ingredients:

- 1 cup rolled oats
- 1 cup almond milk
- 1 tablespoon chia seeds
- 1 cup fresh mixed berries (such as strawberries, blueberries, and raspberries)
- 1 cup low-fat Greek yogurt

Directions:

1. In a bowl, mix the rolled oats, almond milk, and chia seeds. Stir well and let the mixture sit for at least 5 minutes to allow the oats and chia seeds to absorb the almond milk and become slightly soft.

2. In serving glasses or jars, begin to layer your parfait. Start with a layer of the oat mixture, followed by a layer of Greek yogurt.

3. Add a generous layer of fresh mixed berries. Repeat the layering process until all ingredients are used up.

4. Finish with a final layer of berries on top. For an extra touch, sprinkle a few oats or chia seeds on top of the berries.

5. Serve immediately for a fresh breakfast, or cover and refrigerate overnight for an even softer oat texture, ready to enjoy in the morning.

Nutritional Information per serving:
300 calories, 15g protein, 45g carbohydrates, 5g total fat, 7g fiber, 10mg cholesterol, 80mg sodium, 350mg potassium, 12g sugars.

2. Zesty Avocado Toast on Whole Grain

Yield: 2 servings | **Prep time:** 5 minutes | **Cook time:** 2 minutes

Ingredients:

- 1 large avocado, sliced
- 1 teaspoon lemon juice
- 1/4 teaspoon red pepper flakes (adjust to taste)
- 2 slices of whole-grain bread

Directions:

1. Toast the whole-grain bread slices to your preferred level of crispiness using a toaster or a skillet over medium heat.

2. In a small bowl, gently mash the sliced avocado with lemon juice and red pepper flakes. The lemon juice not only adds flavor but also helps prevent the avocado from browning.

3. Spread the mashed avocado evenly over the toasted whole-grain bread slices. Ensure the avocado layer is thick and covers the toast for maximum flavor.

4. If desired, sprinkle a tiny bit more red pepper flakes on top of each toast for an extra kick. Serve immediately to enjoy the toast at its best texture and taste.

Nutritional Information per serving:
250 calories, 9g protein, 35g carbohydrates, 9g total fat, 8g fiber, 0mg cholesterol, 150mg sodium, 400mg potassium, 3g sugars.

3. Vibrant Heart-Healthy Smoothie Bowl

Yield: 2 servings | **Prep time:** 10 minutes | **Cook time:** 0 minutes

Ingredients:

- 1 cup fresh spinach
- 1 cup frozen mixed berries (such as strawberries, blueberries, and raspberries)
- 1 medium banana
- 1 tablespoon flaxseeds
- 1 cup almond milk
- 1/2 cup unsweetened granola

Directions:

1. In a blender, combine the spinach, frozen berries, banana, flaxseeds, and almond milk. Blend on high speed until the mixture is smooth and creamy. Adjust the amount of almond milk to achieve your desired consistency.

2. Pour the smoothie mixture into two bowls. The vibrant color from the berries and spinach not only makes this bowl visually appealing but is also indicative of the rich antioxidants present.

3. Top each bowl with a sprinkle of unsweetened granola, adding a delightful crunch and fiber to your smoothie bowl. For an extra touch of nutrition and flavor, you can also add a few fresh berry slices or a banana slice on top.

4. Serve immediately. Enjoy this heart-healthy smoothie bowl as a nourishing start to your day, knowing you're fueling your body with ingredients that support cardiovascular health and overall well-being.

Nutritional Information per serving:
310 calories, 10g protein, 55g carbohydrates, 7g total fat, 9g fiber, 0mg cholesterol, 70mg sodium, 550mg potassium, 20g sugars.

4. Autumn Harvest Quinoa Fruit Breakfast Cup

Yield: 4 servings | **Prep time:** 15 minutes | **Cook time:** 0 minutes (assuming quinoa is precooked)

Ingredients:

- 2 cups cooked quinoa, cooled
- 1 large apple, diced
- 1/2 cup walnuts, chopped
- 1 teaspoon cinnamon
- 1 cup low-fat milk (or almond milk for a dairy-free option)

Directions:

1. In a large mixing bowl, combine the cooled cooked quinoa, diced apple, and chopped walnuts. Gently toss these ingredients together until well mixed.

2. Sprinkle the cinnamon over the quinoa mixture and stir again to distribute the spice evenly throughout.

3. Divide the quinoa mixture evenly among four breakfast cups or bowls. Pour a quarter cup of low-fat milk over each serving, allowing the quinoa to soak up some of the milk and the flavors to meld.

4. If desired, let the breakfast cups sit for a few minutes before serving to soften the quinoa slightly and intensify the flavors. Alternatively, these cups can be assembled the night before and stored in the refrigerator for an easy, grab-and-go breakfast.

5. Serve each quinoa fruit breakfast cup with an extra sprinkle of cinnamon on top for garnish and a boost of antioxidant-rich spice.

Nutritional Information per serving:
280 calories, 9g protein, 44g carbohydrates, 8g total fat, 6g fiber, 5mg cholesterol, 55mg sodium, 300mg potassium, 15g sugars.

5. Crunchy Almond Bliss Banana Toast

Yield: 2 servings | **Prep time:** 5 minutes | **Cook time:** 2 minutes

Ingredients:

- 2 slices of whole-grain bread
- 2 tablespoons almond butter
- 1 banana, sliced
- 1 teaspoon chia seeds

Directions:

1. Toast the whole-grain bread slices to your preferred level of crunchiness, either in a toaster or on a skillet over medium heat.

2. Spread one tablespoon of almond butter evenly over each slice of toasted bread, ensuring full coverage for a rich, nutty flavor in every bite.

3. Arrange banana slices neatly on top of the almond butter layer, covering the toast surface for a sweet complement to the nutty undertones.

4. Sprinkle half a teaspoon of chia seeds over each toast, adding a delightful crunch and a boost of fiber and omega-3 fatty acids.

5. Serve immediately to enjoy the contrast of warm toast against the cool, creamy banana and almond butter, with a final crunch from the chia seeds.

Nutritional Information per serving:
320 calories, 11g protein, 42g carbohydrates, 14g total fat, 7g fiber, 0mg cholesterol, 200mg sodium, 450mg potassium, 12g sugars.

6. Cozy Cinnamon Blueberry Oatmeal

Yield: 4 servings | **Prep time:** 5 minutes | **Cook time:** 20 minutes

Ingredients:

- 1 cup steel-cut oats
- 4 cups almond milk
- 1/2 cup sliced almonds
- 1 cup blueberries (fresh or frozen)
- A dash of cinnamon (about 1/4 teaspoon)

Directions:

1. In a medium saucepan, bring the almond milk to a boil. Add the steel-cut oats and a dash of cinnamon, then reduce the heat to a simmer.

2. Cook the oats, stirring occasionally, for about 20 minutes, or until the oats have absorbed the almond milk and reached your desired consistency.

3. While the oatmeal is still hot, stir in the blueberries and sliced almonds, reserving a few for topping. The heat from the oatmeal will slightly soften the blueberries, enhancing their sweetness.

4. Divide the oatmeal into bowls. Garnish each serving with the reserved almonds and a few extra blueberries on top for a burst of flavor and color.

5. Serve warm, adding more almond milk if a thinner consistency is preferred. Enjoy the heartwarming blend of flavors, perfect for starting your day on a nutritious note.

Nutritional Information per serving:
290 calories, 10g protein, 49g carbohydrates, 7g total fat, 8g fiber, 0mg cholesterol, 60mg sodium, 200mg potassium, 8g sugars.

7. Mediterranean Spinach and Feta Omelet

Yield: 2 servings | **Prep time:** 10 minutes |
Cook time: 8 minutes

Ingredients:

- 4 large egg whites
- 1 cup fresh spinach, roughly chopped
- 1/4 cup feta cheese, crumbled
- 1/2 cup tomatoes, diced
- 1 tablespoon olive oil

Directions:

1. Heat the olive oil in a non-stick skillet over medium heat. Add the chopped spinach and diced tomatoes, sautéing until the spinach is wilted and the tomatoes are slightly softened, about 2-3 minutes.

2. In a medium bowl, whisk together the egg whites until frothy. Pour the egg whites over the sautéed spinach and tomatoes in the skillet, letting them set for a minute before gently stirring to distribute the spinach and tomatoes evenly.

3. Sprinkle the crumbled feta cheese over half of the omelet. Allow the omelet to cook undisturbed for another 2-3 minutes, or until the eggs are set and the bottom is lightly golden.

4. Carefully fold the omelet in half, covering the feta-filled side. Cook for an additional minute to ensure the feta is slightly melted.

5. Slide the omelet onto a plate, cut in half to serve. Optionally, drizzle with a little more olive oil or sprinkle with additional fresh herbs for enhanced flavor.

Nutritional Information per serving:
180 calories, 18g protein, 6g carbohydrates, 9g total fat, 2g fiber, 0mg cholesterol, 220mg sodium, 300mg potassium, 2g sugars.

8. Aegean Breeze Morning Wrap

Yield: 2 servings | **Prep time:** 10 minutes |
Cook time: 0 minutes

Ingredients:

- 2 whole-wheat wraps
- 4 tablespoons hummus
- 1/2 cucumber, thinly sliced
- 1/2 cup cherry tomatoes, halved
- 1/4 cup olives, sliced
- 1/4 red onion, thinly sliced

Directions:

1. Lay out the whole-wheat wraps on a clean flat surface. Spread 2 tablespoons of hummus evenly over each wrap, leaving a small border around the edges.

2. On one half of each wrap, layer the cucumber slices, cherry tomato halves, sliced olives, and red onion slices. Distribute the vegetables evenly to ensure every bite is flavorful and nutritious.

3. Carefully fold the wrap over the vegetable filling, tucking in the sides as you roll to secure the fillings inside. If needed, you can use a toothpick to help keep the wrap closed.

4. Cut each wrap in half diagonally and serve immediately. Enjoy the refreshing and satisfying combination of flavors that make this wrap a perfect start to your day.

Nutritional Information per serving:
270 calories, 9g protein, 39g carbohydrates, 9g total fat, 6g fiber, 0mg cholesterol, 310mg sodium, 360mg potassium, 4g sugars.

9. Strawberry Vanilla Chia Seed Pudding Bliss

Yield: 4 servings | **Prep time:** 10 minutes | **Cook time:** 0 minutes (Refrigeration time: at least 4 hours or overnight)

Ingredients:

- 1/2 cup chia seeds
- 2 cups almond milk (unsweetened)
- 1 teaspoon vanilla extract
- 1 cup strawberries, hulled and sliced

Directions:

1. In a medium bowl, whisk together the almond milk and vanilla extract. Add the chia seeds and stir until well combined.

2. Let the mixture sit for 5 minutes, then stir again to prevent the chia seeds from clumping together. Cover the bowl with plastic wrap or a lid and refrigerate for at least 4 hours, or overnight, until the pudding has thickened and the chia seeds have absorbed the almond milk, creating a pudding-like consistency.

3. Before serving, give the chia seed pudding a good stir to ensure an even texture. If the pudding is too thick, you can adjust the consistency by adding a little more almond milk and stirring well.

4. Serve the chia seed pudding into individual cups or bowls. Top each serving with a generous layer of sliced strawberries, distributing them evenly among the servings.

5. Enjoy this blissful chia seed pudding as a nourishing start to your day or a refreshing snack. The combination of creamy pudding with the sweetness of strawberries makes for a delightful heart-healthy treat.

Nutritional Information per serving:
210 calories, 7g protein, 24g carbohydrates, 10g total fat, 10g fiber, 0mg cholesterol, 30mg sodium, 150mg potassium, 8g sugars.

10. Sunrise Fiesta Breakfast Burrito

Yield: 2 servings | **Prep time:** 10 minutes | **Cook time:** 10 minutes

Ingredients:

- 2 whole wheat tortillas
- 4 egg whites
- 1/2 cup bell peppers, diced (mix of colors)
- 1/4 cup onions, diced
- 1/2 cup black beans, rinsed and drained
- 1/4 cup salsa, low sodium

Directions:

1. In a non-stick skillet over medium heat, sauté the diced bell peppers and onions until they are soft and slightly caramelized, about 5-7 minutes. Remove from the skillet and set aside.

2. In the same skillet, lightly sprayed with cooking spray or a drop of olive oil, cook the egg whites, scrambling until fully cooked and fluffy, about 3 minutes.

3. Warm the whole wheat tortillas in a microwave for about 10 seconds or in a dry skillet over low heat for 30 seconds on each side.

4. Assemble the burritos by laying out each tortilla on a flat surface. Divide the scrambled egg whites evenly among the tortillas, and top each with half of the sautéed bell peppers and onions, black beans, and salsa.

5. Fold in the sides of each tortilla and roll up tightly to enclose the filling. Cut each burrito in half, if desired, and serve immediately with additional salsa on the side for dipping.

Nutritional Information per serving:
330 calories, 20g protein, 48g carbohydrates, 8g total fat, 8g fiber, 0mg cholesterol, 350mg sodium, 400mg potassium, 5g sugars.

11. Lemon Ricotta Whole Wheat Pancakes

Yield: 4 servings | **Prep time:** 15 minutes |
Cook time: 10 minutes

Ingredients:

- 1 cup whole wheat flour
- 1/2 cup low-fat ricotta cheese
- Zest of 1 lemon
- 2 eggs
- 2 tablespoons honey
- 1 cup water or almond milk (adjust for batter consistency)
- Cooking spray or a teaspoon of olive oil for the pan

Directions:

1. In a large mixing bowl, combine the whole wheat flour, low-fat ricotta cheese, and lemon zest. Stir these dry ingredients together until they are well mixed.

2. In a separate bowl, beat the eggs and then mix in the honey and water or almond milk. Whisk these wet ingredients together until they are fully combined.

3. Pour the wet ingredients into the bowl with the dry ingredients, stirring until just combined. Be careful not to overmix; a few lumps are okay. If the batter is too thick, add a little more water or almond milk to reach your desired consistency.

4. Heat a non-stick skillet or griddle over medium heat and lightly coat with cooking spray or olive oil. Pour 1/4 cup of batter onto the skillet for each pancake. Cook until bubbles form on the surface of the pancake and the edges look set, about 2-3 minutes.

5. Flip the pancakes and cook for an additional 2 minutes on the other side, or until golden brown and cooked through. Repeat with the remaining batter.

6. Serve the pancakes warm, drizzled with a little extra honey or topped with fresh berries for added sweetness and flavor.

Nutritional Information per serving:
280 calories, 14g protein, 46g carbohydrates, 5g total fat, 4g fiber, 93mg cholesterol, 150mg sodium, 90mg potassium, 9g sugars.

12. Morning Vitality Green Juice

Yield: 2 servings | **Prep time:** 10 minutes |
Cook time: 0 minutes

Ingredients:

- 2 cups kale, stems removed
- 1 green apple, cored and sliced
- 1 cucumber, chopped
- Juice of 1 lemon
- 1-inch piece of ginger, peeled

Directions:

1. Rinse all the vegetables and the apple under cold water. Pat dry with a kitchen towel. Prepare the ingredients by removing the stems from the kale, coring and slicing the green apple, chopping the cucumber, and peeling the ginger.

2. In a juicer, start by juicing the kale, followed by the green apple, cucumber, and ginger. This order helps maximize juice extraction and ensures the softer ingredients push through any leftover kale in the juicer.

3. Once all the ingredients have been juiced, stir in the lemon juice directly into the juicer's pitcher or mix it into the juice in a separate container to ensure even distribution.

4. Pour the green juice into two glasses. If desired, you can strain the juice for a smoother texture or enjoy it as is for added fiber.

5. Serve immediately to enjoy the maximum nutritional benefits. This energizing green juice is a refreshing way to kickstart your morning with a burst of nutrients.

Nutritional Information per serving:
120 calories, 4g protein, 28g carbohydrates, 1g total fat, 5g fiber, 0mg cholesterol, 70mg sodium, 490mg potassium, 18g sugars.

13. Sunrise Garden Breakfast Salad

Yield: 2 servings | **Prep time:** 10 minutes | **Cook time:** 5 minutes (for boiling the egg)

Ingredients:

- 2 cups mixed greens (such as spinach, arugula, and romaine)
- 1/2 cup cherry tomatoes, halved
- 1 avocado, peeled, pitted, and sliced
- 1/4 cup walnuts, roughly chopped
- 2 eggs, boiled to your preference
- 2 tablespoons balsamic vinaigrette

Directions:

1. Begin by boiling the eggs to your preferred level of doneness — soft, medium, or hard-boiled. Once cooked, place the eggs in cold water to cool before peeling and slicing them.

2. In a large mixing bowl, combine the mixed greens, cherry tomato halves, and sliced avocado. Toss gently to mix the ingredients.

3. Add the chopped walnuts to the salad mix, providing a crunchy texture and a dose of healthy fats.

4. Drizzle the balsamic vinaigrette over the salad and toss again to ensure all the ingredients are lightly coated with the dressing.

5. Divide the salad into two serving bowls. Top each salad with a sliced boiled egg, placing the egg slices evenly across the salad to distribute the protein throughout.

6. Serve immediately, enjoying the blend of savory flavors and the satisfying combination of textures. This salad offers a fresh, nutritious start to your day, packed with vitamins, minerals, and heart-healthy fats.

Nutritional Information per serving:
310 calories, 13g protein, 15g carbohydrates, 22g total fat, 7g fiber, 186mg cholesterol, 120mg sodium, 450mg potassium, 4g sugars.

14. Peachy Keen Cottage Cheese Delight

Yield: 2 servings | **Prep time:** 5 minutes | **Cook time:** 0 minutes

Ingredients:

- 1 cup low-fat cottage cheese
- 1 peach, sliced
- 1 tablespoon flaxseeds
- A drizzle of honey (about 1 teaspoon)

Directions:

1. Divide the cottage cheese evenly between two bowls. This creamy, high-protein base will hold the rest of your ingredients.

2. Top the cottage cheese with fresh peach slices. If peaches are out of season, you can use thawed frozen peaches or substitute with another soft, sweet fruit like nectarines or mangos.

3. Sprinkle the flaxseeds over the top of each bowl. Flaxseeds not only add a crunchy texture but also provide omega-3 fatty acids, fiber, and antioxidants.

4. Finish each bowl with a drizzle of honey for a touch of natural sweetness that complements the tanginess of the cottage cheese and the freshness of the peaches.

5. Serve immediately and enjoy a refreshing, protein-packed start to your day that's both nourishing and satisfying.

Nutritional Information per serving:
220 calories, 24g protein, 27g carbohydrates, 2g total fat, 3g fiber, 10mg cholesterol, 350mg sodium, 200mg potassium, 16g sugars.

15. Sunrise Millet Fruit Bowl

Yield: 4 servings | **Prep time:** 10 minutes | **Cook time:** 20 minutes (for cooking millet)

Ingredients:

- 1 cup millet
- 2 cups water
- 1 cup mixed fresh fruit (such as berries, kiwi, and orange), chopped
- 1/4 cup slivered almonds

Directions:

1. Rinse the millet under cold water until the water runs clear. In a medium saucepan, bring 2 cups of water to a boil. Add the rinsed millet, reduce the heat to low, cover, and simmer for about 20 minutes, or until the water is absorbed and the millet is tender.

2. Once the millet is cooked, fluff it with a fork and allow it to cool slightly. You can speed up this process by spreading it out on a plate.

3. While the millet is cooling, prepare the fruit by chopping it into bite-sized pieces. This medley of berries, kiwi, and orange will provide a burst of vitamins, antioxidants, and natural sweetness.

4. Divide the cooked millet among four bowls. Top each bowl evenly with the chopped fresh fruit, ensuring a good mix of colors and flavors in each serving.

5. Sprinkle slivered almonds over each bowl for a crunchy texture and a boost of healthy fats.

6. Serve immediately for a warm breakfast or chill the cooked millet before assembling for a refreshing cold cereal alternative.

Nutritional Information per serving:

250 calories, 6g protein, 45g carbohydrates, 5g total fat, 6g fiber, 0mg cholesterol, 10mg sodium, 250mg potassium, 10g sugars.

16. Autumn Glow Pumpkin Spice Muffins

Yield: 6 servings | **Prep time:** 15 minutes | **Cook time:** 20 minutes

Ingredients:

- 2 cups whole wheat flour
- 1 cup pumpkin puree
- 4 egg whites
- 1/2 cup chopped walnuts
- 1 teaspoon cinnamon
- 1/2 teaspoon nutmeg
- 1/4 cup honey (optional for sweetness)
- 1 teaspoon baking powder
- 1/2 teaspoon baking soda
- A pinch of salt

Directions:

1. Preheat your oven to 350°F (175°C). Line a muffin tin with paper liners or lightly grease with cooking spray.

2. In a large bowl, combine the whole wheat flour, baking powder, baking soda, cinnamon, nutmeg, and a pinch of salt. Mix well to distribute the spices evenly.

3. In a separate bowl, whisk together the pumpkin puree, egg whites, and honey (if using) until smooth. Stir in the chopped walnuts.

4. Gradually add the wet ingredients to the dry ingredients, stirring just until combined. Be careful not to overmix to keep the muffins tender.

5. Divide the batter evenly among the muffin cups, filling each about three-quarters full.

6. Bake in the preheated oven for about 20 minutes, or until a toothpick inserted into the center of a muffin comes out clean.

7. Let the muffins cool in the pan for 5 minutes before transferring them to a wire rack to cool completely.

Nutritional Information per serving:

180 calories, 5g protein, 30g carbohydrates, 5g total fat, 4g fiber, 0mg cholesterol, 200mg sodium, 120mg potassium, 12g sugars.

17. Citrus Glow Quinoa Salad

Yield: 4 servings | **Prep time:** 15 minutes |
Cook time: 0 minutes (assuming quinoa is pre-cooked)

Ingredients:

- 2 cups cooked quinoa, cooled
- 1 orange, peeled and segmented
- 1/2 cup pomegranate seeds
- 1/4 cup chopped almonds
- For the lemon dressing:
- 2 tablespoons olive oil
- Juice of 1 lemon
- 1 teaspoon honey (optional)
- Salt and pepper to taste

Directions:

1. In a small bowl, whisk together the olive oil, lemon juice, honey (if using), and a pinch of salt and pepper to create the dressing. Adjust the seasoning according to your taste.

2. In a large mixing bowl, combine the cooled cooked quinoa with the orange segments and pomegranate seeds. Toss gently to mix.

3. Drizzle the lemon dressing over the quinoa mixture and toss again to ensure everything is evenly coated.

4. Just before serving, sprinkle the chopped almonds over the top of the salad for a crunchy texture and a nutty flavor.

5. Divide the salad into individual servings or present it in a large bowl for a colorful and inviting breakfast option.

Nutritional Information per serving:
270 calories, 8g protein, 44g carbohydrates, 7g total fat, 5g fiber, 0mg cholesterol, 30mg sodium, 320mg potassium, 10g sugars.

18. Forest Bounty Spinach and Mushroom Frittata

Yield: 4 servings | **Prep time:** 10 minutes |
Cook time: 15 minutes

Ingredients:

- 8 egg whites
- 1 cup mushrooms, sliced
- 1 cup spinach, chopped
- 1/2 cup low-fat feta cheese, crumbled
- 1 tablespoon mixed herbs (such as parsley, chives, and thyme), finely chopped
- Salt and pepper to taste
- Cooking spray or a teaspoon of olive oil for the pan

Directions:

1. Preheat the oven to 375°F (190°C) if your skillet is oven-safe. If not, you will transfer the frittata to a baking dish for the oven part.

2. In a medium oven-safe skillet, heat a light spray of cooking spray or a drizzle of olive oil over medium heat. Add the sliced mushrooms and sauté until they release their moisture and begin to brown, about 5-7 minutes.

3. Add the chopped spinach to the skillet, stirring until the spinach has wilted, about 2 minutes. Season the vegetables with a pinch of salt and pepper.

4. In a large bowl, whisk the egg whites until frothy. Stir in the crumbled feta cheese and mixed herbs, then pour this mixture over the sautéed vegetables in the skillet. Cook for 3-4 minutes until the edges begin to set.

5. Transfer the skillet to the preheated oven (or into a pre-greased baking dish if your skillet isn't oven-safe) and bake for 8-10 minutes, or until the center is set and the top is lightly golden.

6. Remove from the oven, let it cool for a couple of minutes, then slice into wedges and serve.

Nutritional Information per serving:
140 calories, 20g protein, 5g carbohydrates, 4g total fat, 1g fiber, 0mg cholesterol, 220mg sodium, 400mg potassium, 2g sugars.

19. Sunrise Berry Oat Bran Muffins

Yield: 6 servings | **Prep time:** 15 minutes | **Cook time:** 20 minutes

Ingredients:

- 2 cups oat bran
- 1 cup almond milk (unsweetened)
- 1 cup fresh berries (such as blueberries, raspberries, and strawberries, chopped if large)
- 4 egg whites
- 1/4 cup honey

Directions:

1. Preheat your oven to 375°F (190°C). Line a muffin tin with paper liners or lightly grease it with cooking spray to prevent sticking.

2. In a large mixing bowl, combine the oat bran and almond milk. Let it sit for 5 minutes to allow the oat bran to absorb some of the liquid and soften.

3. In a separate bowl, whisk the egg whites until they are frothy. Then, stir in the honey until it is well incorporated.

4. Add the egg white and honey mixture to the softened oat bran. Stir until just combined. Gently fold in the fresh berries, being careful not to crush them.

5. Divide the batter evenly among the muffin tin cavities, filling each about three-quarters full.

6. Bake in the preheated oven for about 20 minutes, or until the tops of the muffins are golden brown and a toothpick inserted into the center of a muffin comes out clean.

7. Allow the muffins to cool in the pan for 5 minutes before transferring them to a wire rack to cool completely.

Nutritional Information per serving:
150 calories, 6g protein, 28g carbohydrates, 2g total fat, 5g fiber, 0mg cholesterol, 80mg sodium, 90mg potassium, 8g sugars.

20. Island Sunrise Smoothie

Yield: 2 servings | **Prep time:** 5 minutes | **Cook time:** 0 minutes

Ingredients:

- 1 cup spinach, fresh
- 1 cup frozen mango chunks
- 1 ripe banana
- 2 cups coconut water
- 1 tablespoon ground flaxseed

Directions:

1. In a blender, combine the fresh spinach, frozen mango chunks, ripe banana, coconut water, and ground flaxseed.

2. Blend on high speed until the mixture is smooth and creamy. If the smoothie is too thick for your liking, you can add a little more coconut water to reach your desired consistency.

3. Once fully blended, taste the smoothie. If you prefer it a bit sweeter, you can add a touch of honey or agave syrup (this may alter the nutritional content slightly).

4. Pour the smoothie into two glasses, dividing evenly. For an extra touch of tropical flair, garnish each glass with a small slice of mango or a banana slice on the rim.

5. Serve immediately to enjoy the refreshing and energizing benefits of this tropical morning treat.

Nutritional Information per serving:
220 calories, 5g protein, 45g carbohydrates, 3g total fat, 7g fiber, 0mg cholesterol, 40mg sodium, 600mg potassium, 20g sugars.

Revitalizing Lunches: Meals to Power Through Your Day

1. Heart-Healthy Mediterranean Bowl

Yield: 4 servings | **Prep time:** 15 minutes | **Cook time:** 20 minutes

Ingredients:

- 1 cup quinoa
- 1 can (15 oz) chickpeas, rinsed and drained
- 1 cucumber, diced
- 1 cup cherry tomatoes, halved
- 1/2 cup olives, sliced
- 1/2 cup feta cheese, crumbled
- For the lemon vinaigrette:
- 3 tablespoons olive oil
- Juice of 1 lemon
- 1 garlic clove, minced
- Salt and pepper to taste

Directions:

1. Cook the quinoa according to package instructions. Fluff with a fork and let cool.

2. In a large bowl, combine the cooled quinoa, chickpeas, diced cucumber, cherry tomatoes, and sliced olives.

3. In a small bowl, whisk together the olive oil, lemon juice, minced garlic, salt, and pepper to create the lemon vinaigrette. Adjust seasoning to taste.

4. Pour the lemon vinaigrette over the quinoa mixture and toss to combine. Ensure all ingredients are evenly coated with the dressing.

5. Divide the salad among four bowls. Sprinkle crumbled feta cheese over each serving.

6. Serve immediately, or chill in the refrigerator for 30 minutes before serving for enhanced flavors.

Nutritional Information per serving:
350 calories, 14g protein, 55g carbohydrates, 9g total fat, 12g fiber, 0mg cholesterol, 200mg sodium, 450mg potassium, 6g sugars.

2. Avocado Chicken Salad Wrap

Yield: 4 servings | **Prep time:** 20 minutes | **Cook time:** 10 minutes

Ingredients:

- 2 grilled chicken breasts, sliced or shredded
- 1 ripe avocado, mashed
- 1/2 cup celery, finely chopped
- 4 whole grain wraps
- 2 cups mixed greens

Directions:

1. Grill the chicken breasts until fully cooked, about 5 minutes on each side, depending on thickness. Allow them to cool slightly before slicing or shredding.

2. In a medium bowl, combine the mashed avocado and chopped celery. Mix well until the celery is evenly distributed through the avocado.

3. Lay out the whole grain wraps on a flat surface. Spread the avocado and celery mixture evenly across each wrap, leaving a small border around the edges.

4. Add the grilled chicken on top of the avocado layer. Then, add a handful of mixed greens to each wrap.

5. Carefully roll up each wrap, folding in the sides first to enclose the filling, then rolling tightly from one end to the other. Cut each wrap in half diagonally before serving.

Nutritional Information per serving:
300 calories, 25g protein, 25g carbohydrates, 8g total fat, 7g fiber, 60mg cholesterol, 250mg sodium, 500mg potassium, 3g sugars.

3. Rainbow Quinoa Veggie Stir-Fry

Yield: 4 servings | **Prep time:** 15 minutes | **Cook time:** 15 minutes

Ingredients:

- 2 cups cooked quinoa
- 1 cup broccoli florets
- 1 bell pepper, julienned (preferably red or yellow for color)
- 1 cup carrots, julienned
- 2 tablespoons low-sodium soy sauce
- 1 tablespoon fresh ginger, minced

Directions:

1. Prepare the quinoa according to package instructions, if not already cooked. Set aside to cool.

2. Heat a large skillet or wok over medium-high heat. Add the broccoli, bell pepper, and carrots, sautéing until just tender but still crisp, about 5-7 minutes. Stir frequently to ensure even cooking.

3. Add the minced ginger to the vegetables and cook for an additional minute, allowing the fragrance to release.

4. Reduce the heat to medium. Stir in the cooked quinoa and low-sodium soy sauce, mixing thoroughly to combine all the ingredients. Cook for another 2-3 minutes, or until everything is heated through.

5. Taste and adjust seasoning if necessary. Serve immediately.

Nutritional Information per serving:
280 calories, 10g protein, 45g carbohydrates, 5g total fat, 8g fiber, 0mg cholesterol, 220mg sodium, 400mg potassium, 8g sugars.

4. Nourishing Lentil and Spinach Soup

Yield: 4 servings | **Prep time:** 10 minutes | **Cook time:** 30 minutes

Ingredients:

- 1 cup lentils, rinsed
- 4 cups low-sodium vegetable broth
- 2 cups spinach, roughly chopped
- 1 cup carrots, diced
- 1 cup onions, diced
- 2 cloves garlic, minced

Directions:

1. In a large pot over medium heat, sauté the onions and garlic until the onions are translucent and fragrant, about 3-5 minutes.

2. Add the diced carrots to the pot and cook for an additional 5 minutes, or until slightly softened.

3. Pour the low-sodium vegetable broth into the pot and bring to a boil. Add the rinsed lentils, reduce the heat to low, cover, and simmer for about 20 minutes, or until the lentils are tender.

4. Stir in the chopped spinach and cook until the spinach has wilted and is fully integrated into the soup, about 3 minutes.

5. Remove from heat and serve hot. For a smoother texture, you can blend part of the soup before adding the spinach, then combine for a mixed texture.

Nutritional Information per serving:
210 calories, 14g protein, 35g carbohydrates, 1g total fat, 15g fiber, 0mg cholesterol, 140mg sodium, 600mg potassium, 4g sugars.

5. Refreshing Tuna Salad Stuffed Avocado

Yield: 4 servings | **Prep time:** 15 minutes | **Cook time:** 0 minutes

Ingredients:

- 2 cans of tuna in water (5 oz each), drained
- 2 avocados, halved and pitted
- 1/4 cup red onion, finely chopped
- 1/4 cup Greek yogurt
- 2 tablespoons lemon juice
- Salt and pepper to taste

Directions:

1. In a medium bowl, mix the drained tuna, chopped red onion, Greek yogurt, and lemon juice. Stir until all ingredients are well combined. Season with salt and pepper according to your taste.

2. Scoop out some of the avocado flesh to create more space for the filling, leaving a thick border around the edges to maintain the structure. Chop the scooped avocado flesh and stir it into the tuna mixture.

3. Fill the avocado halves with the tuna salad mixture, distributing it evenly among the four halves.

4. Optionally, garnish with additional chopped red onion or a sprinkle of paprika for color and flavor.

5. Serve immediately as a light yet satisfying lunch that combines healthy fats, protein, and the refreshing zest of lemon.

Nutritional Information per serving:
320 calories, 25g protein, 20g carbohydrates, 15g total fat, 7g fiber, 0mg cholesterol, 180mg sodium, 500mg potassium, 3g sugars.

6. Garden Delight Grilled Veggie and Hummus Sandwich

Yield: 4 servings | **Prep time:** 15 minutes | **Cook time:** 10 minutes

Ingredients:

- 8 slices of whole grain bread
- 1 cup hummus
- 1 medium zucchini, sliced lengthwise
- 1 medium eggplant, sliced into rounds
- 1 large red bell pepper, sliced into wide strips

Directions:

1. Preheat your grill or grill pan over medium heat. Lightly brush the zucchini, eggplant, and red bell pepper slices with olive oil and season with salt and pepper to taste.

2. Grill the vegetables in batches, turning once, until they are tender and have nice grill marks, about 3-4 minutes per side for the zucchini and eggplant, and 5-6 minutes per side for the bell pepper.

3. Spread hummus generously on one side of each slice of whole grain bread. Arrange the grilled vegetables evenly over four of the slices.

4. Top the vegetables with the remaining bread slices, hummus side down, to make four sandwiches.

5. If desired, you can cut each sandwich in half for easier eating. Serve immediately while the vegetables are still warm, or pack for a nutritious lunch on the go.

Nutritional Information per serving:
260 calories, 9g protein, 40g carbohydrates, 7g total fat, 12g fiber, 0mg cholesterol, 300mg sodium, 450mg potassium, 10g sugars.

7. Autumn Harvest Kale and Sweet Potato Salad

Yield: 4 servings | **Prep time:** 15 minutes | **Cook time:** 25 minutes

Ingredients:

- 4 cups kale, stemmed and chopped
- 2 medium sweet potatoes, peeled and diced
- 1/4 cup dried cranberries
- 1/4 cup walnuts, chopped
- 1/4 cup balsamic vinaigrette

Directions:

1. Preheat the oven to 400°F (200°C). Toss the diced sweet potatoes with a drizzle of olive oil and a pinch of salt. Spread them out on a baking sheet and roast in the oven until tender and slightly caramelized, about 25 minutes.

2. While the sweet potatoes are roasting, prepare the kale by washing, stemming, and chopping it into bite-sized pieces. If desired, massage the kale with a little olive oil to soften the leaves.

3. Once the sweet potatoes are done, let them cool slightly. Then, in a large salad bowl, combine the roasted sweet potatoes, prepared kale, dried cranberries, and chopped walnuts.

4. Drizzle the salad with balsamic vinaigrette and toss gently to combine all the ingredients evenly.

5. Serve the salad at room temperature or chilled, as preferred. Adjust seasoning with salt and pepper to taste before serving.

Nutritional Information per serving:
330 calories, 6g protein, 50g carbohydrates, 10g total fat, 8g fiber, 0mg cholesterol, 200mg sodium, 600mg potassium, 12g sugars.

8. Summer Fresh Tomato Basil Zucchini Noodles

Yield: 4 servings | **Prep time:** 15 minutes | **Cook time:** 5 minutes

Ingredients:

- 4 medium zucchinis, spiralized into noodles
- 1 cup cherry tomatoes, halved
- 1/4 cup fresh basil leaves, torn
- 2 tablespoons olive oil
- 2 cloves garlic, minced

Directions:

1. Heat the olive oil in a large skillet over medium heat. Add the minced garlic and sauté for about 1 minute, or until fragrant but not browned.

2. Add the zucchini noodles (zoodles) to the skillet and toss for 2-3 minutes, or until just tender. Be careful not to overcook to maintain a bit of crunch.

3. Remove the skillet from the heat. Gently toss in the cherry tomatoes and fresh basil, allowing the residual heat to warm them without losing their texture.

4. Season the dish with salt and pepper to taste, and divide among serving plates.

5. Optional: For an extra touch of flavor, sprinkle with grated Parmesan or a squeeze of lemon juice before serving.

Nutritional Information per serving:
190 calories, 4g protein, 25g carbohydrates, 9g total fat, 5g fiber, 0mg cholesterol, 80mg sodium, 450mg potassium, 6g sugars.

9. Wholesome Heart-Friendly Bean and Rice Burrito

Yield: 4 servings | **Prep time:** 10 minutes | **Cook time:** 25 minutes (for cooking rice, if not pre-cooked)

Ingredients:

- 2 cups cooked brown rice
- 1 can (15 oz) black beans, rinsed and drained
- 4 whole wheat tortillas
- 1 cup salsa
- 1 avocado, sliced

Directions:

1. Prepare the brown rice according to package instructions if not already cooked. Allow it to cool slightly before assembling the burritos.

2. Warm the whole wheat tortillas in a dry skillet or microwave for about 10-15 seconds each to make them more pliable.

3. Lay out the tortillas on a flat surface. Spread an equal amount of cooked brown rice across the center of each tortilla, leaving room at the edges for folding.

4. Top the rice with black beans, then add a generous spoonful of salsa on top of the beans. Arrange avocado slices over the salsa.

5. Fold in the sides of each tortilla and roll tightly to enclose the filling. If desired, you can lightly grill the burritos in a skillet to crisp the outside and warm the filling.

6. Serve immediately, accompanied by extra salsa or a side salad for a complete meal.

Nutritional Information per serving:
350 calories, 15g protein, 60g carbohydrates, 8g total fat, 15g fiber, 0mg cholesterol, 220mg sodium, 550mg potassium, 5g sugars.

10. Summer Breeze Cucumber Gazpacho

Yield: 4 servings | **Prep time:** 15 minutes | **Cook time:** 0 minutes

Ingredients:

- 2 large cucumbers, peeled and chopped
- 1 large red bell pepper, seeded and chopped
- 1 small onion, peeled and chopped
- 1 clove garlic, minced
- 2 tablespoons white wine vinegar
- 2 tablespoons olive oil
- Salt and pepper to taste
- Ice water, as needed for consistency

Directions:

1. In a blender or food processor, combine the cucumbers, red bell pepper, onion, and garlic. Blend until the mixture reaches your desired consistency, either smooth or slightly chunky.

2. Add the white wine vinegar and olive oil to the vegetable mixture. Blend again to incorporate the liquids thoroughly. Season with salt and pepper to taste.

3. If the gazpacho is thicker than you prefer, gradually add ice water and blend until you achieve the desired consistency. The ice water will also help chill the soup further.

4. Chill the gazpacho in the refrigerator for at least an hour before serving to allow the flavors to meld together.

5. Serve cold, garnished with additional chopped cucumber, bell pepper, or a drizzle of olive oil if desired.

Nutritional Information per serving:
120 calories, 2g protein, 18g carbohydrates, 5g total fat, 4g fiber, 0mg cholesterol, 60mg sodium, 360mg potassium, 8g sugars.

11. Greens & Mushroom Whole Wheat Pasta Delight

Yield: 4 servings | **Prep time:** 10 minutes | **Cook time:** 20 minutes

Ingredients:

- 8 ounces whole wheat pasta
- 2 cups fresh spinach
- 1 cup mushrooms, sliced
- 2 tablespoons olive oil
- 2 cloves garlic, minced

Directions:

1. Cook the whole wheat pasta according to package instructions until al dente. Drain and set aside, reserving a little pasta water for later.

2. In a large skillet, heat the olive oil over medium heat. Add the minced garlic and sauté for about 1 minute or until fragrant.

3. Add the sliced mushrooms to the skillet and cook for 5-7 minutes, or until they have released their moisture and are golden brown.

4. Stir in the fresh spinach and cook until just wilted, about 2-3 minutes.

5. Toss the cooked pasta with the sautéed vegetables in the skillet. If the mixture seems dry, add a bit of the reserved pasta water to help combine everything smoothly.

6. Serve immediately, garnished with additional fresh spinach leaves or a sprinkle of grated Parmesan cheese if desired.

Nutritional Information per serving:
310 calories, 12g protein, 52g carbohydrates, 7g total fat, 10g fiber, 0mg cholesterol, 90mg sodium, 420mg potassium, 4g sugars.

12. Orchard Fresh Crunchy Apple and Walnut Salad

Yield: 4 servings | **Prep time:** 15 minutes | **Cook time:** 0 minutes

Ingredients:

- 6 cups mixed greens (such as spinach, arugula, and romaine)
- 2 apples, cored and thinly sliced
- 1/2 cup walnuts, roughly chopped
- 1/2 cup feta cheese, crumbled
- For the apple cider vinaigrette:
  - 1/4 cup apple cider vinegar
  - 1/2 cup olive oil
  - 2 tablespoons honey
  - Salt and pepper to taste

Directions:

1. In a small bowl, whisk together the apple cider vinegar, olive oil, honey, salt, and pepper until well combined to make the apple cider vinaigrette.

2. In a large salad bowl, combine the mixed greens, apple slices, chopped walnuts, and crumbled feta cheese.

3. Drizzle the apple cider vinaigrette over the salad and toss gently to ensure all ingredients are evenly coated.

4. Serve immediately, offering additional dressing on the side if desired.

Nutritional Information per serving: 290 calories, 7g protein, 40g carbohydrates, 12g total fat, 6g fiber, 0mg cholesterol, 250mg sodium, 320mg potassium, 15g sugars.

13. Savory Balsamic Glazed Brussels Sprouts and Quinoa

Yield: 4 servings | **Prep time:** 15 minutes | **Cook time:** 25 minutes

Ingredients:

- 1 cup quinoa
- 2 cups water
- 1 pound Brussels sprouts, trimmed and halved
- 3 tablespoons olive oil, divided
- 2 tablespoons balsamic vinegar
- 1/4 cup pine nuts

Directions:

1. Rinse the quinoa under cold running water. In a medium saucepan, bring 2 cups of water to a boil. Add the quinoa, reduce the heat to low, cover, and simmer for about 15 minutes, or until the water is absorbed and the quinoa is tender. Fluff with a fork and set aside.

2. While the quinoa is cooking, heat 2 tablespoons of olive oil in a large skillet over medium-high heat. Add the Brussels sprouts, cut side down, and cook without stirring for about 5 minutes, until the undersides turn golden and caramelized.

3. Reduce the heat to medium-low, flip the Brussels sprouts, and add the balsamic vinegar and remaining tablespoon of olive oil. Cover and cook for another 10 minutes, or until the Brussels sprouts are tender. Season with salt and pepper to taste.

4. Toast the pine nuts in a dry skillet over medium heat for about 3 minutes, or until golden and fragrant, stirring frequently to prevent burning.

5. To assemble, mix the cooked quinoa and glazed Brussels sprouts in a large bowl. Sprinkle with toasted pine nuts before serving.

Nutritional Information per serving: 270 calories, 10g protein, 40g carbohydrates, 8g total fat, 9g fiber, 0mg cholesterol, 90mg sodium, 480mg potassium, 5g sugars.

14. Sunshine Mediterranean Chickpea Salad

Yield: 4 servings | **Prep time:** 15 minutes | **Cook time:** 0 minutes

Ingredients:

- 2 cans (15 oz each) chickpeas, rinsed and drained
- 1 cucumber, diced
- 1/2 cup olives, halved
- 1 cup cherry tomatoes, halved
- 1/2 cup feta cheese, crumbled
- For the lemon vinaigrette:
  - 1/4 cup olive oil
  - Juice of 1 lemon
  - 1 teaspoon honey
  - Salt and pepper to taste

Directions:

1. In a large salad bowl, combine the chickpeas, diced cucumber, halved olives, and cherry tomatoes.

2. In a small bowl or jar, whisk together the olive oil, lemon juice, honey, salt, and pepper until well combined and emulsified to make the lemon vinaigrette.

3. Pour the lemon vinaigrette over the salad ingredients and toss gently to ensure everything is evenly coated.

4. Sprinkle the crumbled feta cheese over the top of the salad.

5. Serve immediately or chill in the refrigerator for 30 minutes before serving to allow the flavors to meld together.

Nutritional Information per serving: 320 calories, 14g protein, 45g carbohydrates, 10g total fat, 12g fiber, 0mg cholesterol, 300mg sodium, 450mg potassium, 8g sugars.

15. Harvest Medley Roasted Vegetable Wrap

Yield: 4 servings | **Prep time:** 15 minutes | **Cook time:** 25 minutes

Ingredients:

- 4 whole wheat wraps
- 1 medium eggplant, sliced into rounds
- 1 medium zucchini, sliced into rounds
- 1 bell pepper, sliced into strips
- 1/2 cup hummus

Directions:

1. Preheat the oven to 400°F (200°C). Arrange the eggplant, zucchini, and bell pepper slices on a baking sheet. Lightly brush the vegetables with olive oil and season with salt and pepper.

2. Roast the vegetables in the preheated oven for about 20-25 minutes, or until tender and slightly caramelized, turning halfway through the cooking time.

3. Warm the whole wheat wraps slightly in the oven or on a skillet to make them more pliable.

4. Spread a layer of hummus on each wrap, leaving a small border around the edges.

5. Evenly distribute the roasted vegetables among the wraps, laying them down the center.

6. Roll up the wraps tightly, tucking in the sides as you go to enclose the filling.

7. Cut each wrap in half diagonally and serve warm.

Nutritional Information per serving:
280 calories, 9g protein, 42g carbohydrates, 9g total fat, 10g fiber, 0mg cholesterol, 320mg sodium, 500mg potassium, 6g sugars.

16. Fiery Lentil and Tomato Soup

Yield: 4 servings | **Prep time:** 10 minutes | **Cook time:** 30 minutes

Ingredients:

- 1 cup lentils, rinsed
- 1 can (14 oz) diced tomatoes, undrained
- 1 large onion, diced
- 4 cups low-sodium vegetable broth
- 1 teaspoon chili powder

Directions:

1. In a large pot, heat a splash of water or vegetable broth over medium heat. Add the diced onion and sauté until soft and translucent, about 5 minutes. If the onion starts to stick, add a little more water or broth.

2. Stir in the chili powder and cook for another minute, allowing the spice to become fragrant.

3. Add the rinsed lentils, diced tomatoes with their juice, and vegetable broth to the pot. Bring the mixture to a boil.

4. Once boiling, reduce the heat to a simmer and cover the pot. Let the soup cook for about 25-30 minutes, or until the lentils are tender and the flavors have melded together.

5. Taste and adjust the seasoning as needed, adding more chili powder if you prefer a spicier soup.

6. Serve hot, garnished with fresh cilantro or a dollop of yogurt if desired.

Nutritional Information per serving:
210 calories, 13g protein, 38g carbohydrates, 1g total fat, 14g fiber, 0mg cholesterol, 130mg sodium, 610mg potassium, 6g sugars.

17. Golden Curried Cauliflower Rice

Yield: 4 servings | **Prep time:** 15 minutes | **Cook time:** 10 minutes

Ingredients:

- 4 cups cauliflower rice
- 1 cup peas (fresh or frozen and thawed)
- 1 cup carrots, diced
- 2 teaspoons curry powder
- 1/4 cup almonds, slivered

Directions:

1. Heat a large skillet over medium heat. Add the cauliflower rice and sauté for about 5 minutes, stirring occasionally, until it begins to soften.

2. Add the diced carrots to the skillet and continue to cook for another 3 minutes, or until the carrots start to soften.

3. Stir in the peas and curry powder, mixing well to ensure the cauliflower rice and vegetables are evenly coated with the curry powder. Cook for an additional 2 minutes, or until the peas are heated through.

4. Toast the slivered almonds in a dry pan over medium heat until they are golden and fragrant. Watch them closely to prevent burning.

5. Serve the curried cauliflower rice garnished with toasted almonds on top.

Nutritional Information per serving:
180 calories, 6g protein, 30g carbohydrates, 5g total fat, 8g fiber, 0mg cholesterol, 200mg sodium, 350mg potassium, 5g sugars.

18. Zen Garden Tofu Salad

Yield: 4 servings | **Prep time:** 20 minutes | **Cook time:** 0 minutes

Ingredients:

- 14 oz block of firm tofu, pressed and cubed
- 4 cups mixed greens
- 1 cup mandarin oranges, drained if canned
- 1/4 cup almonds, slivered
- For the low-sodium soy sauce dressing:
  - 2 tablespoons low-sodium soy sauce
  - 2 tablespoons rice vinegar
  - 1 tablespoon sesame oil
  - 1 teaspoon honey
  - 1 garlic clove, minced

Directions:

1. To prepare the dressing, whisk together low-sodium soy sauce, rice vinegar, sesame oil, honey, and minced garlic in a small bowl until well combined. Set aside.

2. In a large salad bowl, combine the mixed greens, cubed tofu, and mandarin oranges.

3. Drizzle the prepared dressing over the salad and toss gently to ensure all ingredients are evenly coated.

4. Sprinkle the slivered almonds over the top of the salad for added crunch.

5. Serve immediately, offering extra dressing on the side if desired.

Nutritional Information per serving:
260 calories, 14g protein, 35g carbohydrates, 9g total fat, 7g fiber, 0mg cholesterol, 220mg sodium, 300mg potassium, 12g sugars.

19. Ocean Breeze Smoked Salmon and Avocado Salad

Yield: 4 servings | **Prep time:** 15 minutes | **Cook time:** 0 minutes

Ingredients:

- 8 oz smoked salmon, thinly sliced
- 2 avocados, sliced
- 6 cups mixed greens
- 2 tablespoons capers, rinsed
- For the lemon dressing:
  - Juice of 1 lemon
  - 3 tablespoons olive oil
  - 1 teaspoon honey
  - Salt and pepper to taste

Directions:

1. In a small bowl, whisk together the lemon juice, olive oil, honey, and a pinch of salt and pepper to create the dressing. Adjust the seasoning according to your taste.

2. Arrange the mixed greens on a large platter or divide them among individual serving plates.

3. Layer the smoked salmon slices and avocado slices over the greens.

4. Scatter the capers evenly over the salad.

5. Drizzle the prepared lemon dressing over the salad just before serving.

6. Serve immediately, enjoying the harmony of flavors that mimic the freshness of the sea paired with the creaminess of avocado.

Nutritional Information per serving:
300 calories, 20g protein, 20g carbohydrates, 15g total fat, 8g fiber, 0mg cholesterol, 320mg sodium, 550mg potassium, 4g sugars.

20. Garden Crisp Veggie Hummus Flatbread

Yield: 4 servings | **Prep time:** 10 minutes | **Cook time:** 5 minutes

Ingredients:

- 4 whole wheat flatbreads
- 1 cup hummus
- 2 cups arugula
- 1 cup cherry tomatoes, halved
- 1/4 cup red onion, thinly sliced

Directions:

1. Preheat your oven to 350°F (175°C). Place the whole wheat flatbreads on a baking sheet and warm in the oven for about 3-5 minutes, just to lightly toast them.

2. Spread a generous layer of hummus over each flatbread, leaving a small border around the edges.

3. Top each flatbread with an even distribution of arugula, cherry tomato halves, and thinly sliced red onion.

4. Optionally, you can return the flatbreads to the oven for an additional 2-3 minutes if you prefer the arugula slightly wilted.

5. Slice each flatbread into wedges and serve immediately, offering a fresh and flavorful meal that combines the hearty base of whole wheat with the vibrancy of fresh veggies and the creamy texture of hummus.

Nutritional Information per serving:
280 calories, 12g protein, 42g carbohydrates, 8g total fat, 9g fiber, 0mg cholesterol, 310mg sodium, 360mg potassium, 6g sugars.

21. Zesty Citrus Shrimp and Avocado Salad

Yield: 4 servings | **Prep time:** 20 minutes | **Cook time:** 5 minutes

Ingredients:

- 4 cups mixed greens
- 1 pound cooked shrimp, peeled and deveined
- 1 avocado, sliced
- 2 oranges, peeled and segmented
- For the lime dressing:
  - Juice of 2 limes
  - 3 tablespoons olive oil
  - 1 tablespoon honey
  - Salt and pepper to taste

Directions:

1. In a small bowl, whisk together the lime juice, olive oil, honey, salt, and pepper to create the dressing. Adjust the seasoning as needed.

2. In a large salad bowl, combine the mixed greens, cooked shrimp, sliced avocado, and orange segments.

3. Drizzle the prepared lime dressing over the salad and gently toss to ensure all ingredients are evenly coated.

4. Divide the salad among serving plates, making sure each plate has a good mix of shrimp, avocado, and orange segments.

5. Serve immediately, offering a refreshing and protein-packed meal that perfectly balances the creamy texture of avocado with the citrusy tang of oranges and lime dressing.

Nutritional Information per serving:
290 calories, 25g protein, 22g carbohydrates, 12g total fat, 7g fiber, 0mg cholesterol, 240mg sodium, 470mg potassium, 6g sugars.

22. Earthy Roasted Beet and Goat Cheese Salad

Yield: 4 servings | **Prep time:** 15 minutes | **Cook time:** 45 minutes for roasting beets

Ingredients:

- 4 medium beets, scrubbed, tops trimmed
- 6 cups mixed greens
- 1/2 cup goat cheese, crumbled
- 1/4 cup walnuts, chopped
- 1/4 cup balsamic reduction

Directions:

1. Preheat your oven to 400°F (200°C). Wrap each beet individually in aluminum foil and place them on a baking sheet. Roast in the preheated oven until the beets are tender and can be easily pierced with a fork, about 45 minutes to 1 hour. Remove from the oven and let cool before peeling and slicing into wedges.

2. While the beets are cooling, place the mixed greens in a large salad bowl.

3. Add the roasted beet wedges to the salad greens. Sprinkle the crumbled goat cheese and chopped walnuts over the top.

4. Drizzle the balsamic reduction over the salad just before serving.

5. Gently toss the salad to mix the ingredients, being careful not to break up the beets too much.

Nutritional Information per serving:
260 calories, 8g protein, 25g carbohydrates, 15g total fat, 6g fiber, 0mg cholesterol, 260mg sodium, 520mg potassium, 9g sugars.

23. Lean Turkey and Spinach Whole Wheat Pita Pocket

Yield: 4 servings | **Prep time:** 20 minutes | **Cook time:** 10 minutes (if cooking turkey breast)

Ingredients:

- 4 whole wheat pita breads
- 1 pound lean turkey breast, cooked and sliced
- 2 cups spinach leaves
- 1 cucumber, thinly sliced
- 1/2 cup tzatziki sauce

Directions:

1. If the turkey breast is not pre-cooked, season it with salt and pepper, and grill or pan-fry until fully cooked and juicy. Let it cool slightly before slicing.

2. Cut the whole wheat pita breads in half to open the pockets. Gently open each pita half to prepare for filling.

3. Layer the sliced turkey breast, spinach leaves, and cucumber slices inside each pita pocket.

4. Spoon a generous amount of tzatziki sauce over the fillings in each pita pocket.

5. Serve immediately, or wrap in foil and warm in an oven preheated to 350°F (175°C) for about 5 minutes if desired.

Nutritional Information per serving:
310 calories, 25g protein, 40g carbohydrates, 6g total fat, 8g fiber, 0mg cholesterol, 280mg sodium, 400mg potassium, 4g sugars.

24. Cozy Autumn Butternut Squash and Black Bean Chili

Yield: 4 servings | **Prep time:** 20 minutes | **Cook time:** 40 minutes

Ingredients:

- 2 cups cubed butternut squash
- 1 can (15 oz) black beans, drained and rinsed
- 1 can (14.5 oz) diced tomatoes, with juice
- 2 tablespoons chili powder
- 1 teaspoon ground cumin
- 1/4 cup fresh cilantro, chopped
- Salt and pepper to taste

Directions:

1. In a large pot over medium heat, add the butternut squash and a splash of water. Cook until slightly tender, about 10 minutes, stirring occasionally.

2. Stir in the black beans, diced tomatoes (with their juice), chili powder, and ground cumin. Season with salt and pepper.

3. Bring the chili to a simmer, then reduce the heat to low. Cover and let cook for about 30 minutes, or until the squash is completely tender and the flavors have melded.

4. Before serving, adjust seasoning to taste and stir in the fresh cilantro.

5. Serve hot, garnished with more cilantro, avocado slices, or a dollop of sour cream if desired.

Nutritional Information per serving:
240 calories, 12g protein, 50g carbohydrates, 1g total fat, 13g fiber, 0mg cholesterol, 220mg sodium, 600mg potassium, 7g sugars.

25. Savory Grilled Portobello Mushroom Burger

Yield: 4 servings | **Prep time:** 10 minutes | **Cook time:** 8 minutes

Ingredients:

- 4 large Portobello mushroom caps
- 4 whole wheat buns
- 4 lettuce leaves
- 1 large tomato, sliced
- 1 small red onion, thinly sliced
- 1 ripe avocado, mashed with a pinch of salt and lemon juice

Directions:

1. Preheat your grill to medium-high heat. Clean the Portobello mushrooms with a damp cloth, remove the stems, and scrape out the gills with a spoon. Brush both sides of the mushrooms with olive oil and season with salt and pepper.

2. Grill the mushroom caps, starting gill-side down, for about 4 minutes on each side, or until they are tender and have grill marks.

3. While the mushrooms are grilling, toast the whole wheat buns on the grill for about 1 minute, or until lightly crispy.

4. To assemble the burgers, spread the mashed avocado on the bottom halves of the buns. Place a grilled mushroom cap on each, followed by a lettuce leaf, tomato slices, and onion slices. Top with the other half of the bun.

5. Serve immediately, offering a delicious and hearty plant-based burger option.

Nutritional Information per serving:
320 calories, 15g protein, 45g carbohydrates, 9g total fat, 10g fiber, 0mg cholesterol, 300mg sodium, 410mg potassium, 8g sugars.

26. Vibrant Zesty Quinoa and Bean Salad

Yield: 4 servings | **Prep time:** 15 minutes | **Cook time:** 20 minutes

Ingredients:

- 1 cup quinoa
- 1 can (15 oz) kidney beans, rinsed and drained
- 1 cup corn (fresh, frozen and thawed, or canned and drained)
- 1 red bell pepper, diced
- For the lime vinaigrette:
  - Juice of 2 limes
  - 1/4 cup olive oil
  - 1 teaspoon honey (adjust to taste)
  - Salt and pepper to taste
- 1/4 cup fresh cilantro, chopped

Directions:

1. Rinse the quinoa under cold water. In a medium saucepan, combine the quinoa with 2 cups of water. Bring to a boil, then reduce heat to low, cover, and simmer for about 15 minutes, or until the quinoa is tender and the water is absorbed. Fluff with a fork and let cool.

2. In a large bowl, combine the cooled quinoa, kidney beans, corn, and diced red bell pepper.

3. In a small bowl, whisk together the lime juice, olive oil, honey, salt, and pepper to create the lime vinaigrette.

4. Pour the vinaigrette over the quinoa mixture and toss to coat evenly.

5. Stir in the chopped cilantro just before serving. Adjust seasoning with salt and pepper if needed.

6. Serve chilled or at room temperature.

Nutritional Information per serving:
270 calories, 14g protein, 52g carbohydrates, 3g total fat, 10g fiber, 0mg cholesterol, 85mg sodium, 430mg potassium, 5g sugars.

Satisfying Dinners: Nourishing Nights for a Strong Heart

1. Zesty Lemon-Herb Baked Salmon

Yield: 4 servings | **Prep time:** 10 minutes | **Cook time:** 15 minutes

Ingredients:

- 4 salmon fillets (6 oz each)
- Juice of 2 lemons
- 2 tablespoons olive oil
- 2 tablespoons fresh dill, chopped
- 2 garlic cloves, minced
- Salt and pepper to taste

Directions:

1. Preheat the oven to 400°F (200°C). Line a baking sheet with parchment paper or lightly grease it.

2. In a small bowl, whisk together lemon juice, olive oil, chopped dill, and minced garlic. Season with salt and pepper.

3. Place the salmon fillets on the prepared baking sheet. Spoon the lemon-herb mixture over each fillet, ensuring they are well coated.

4. Bake in the preheated oven for about 12-15 minutes, or until the salmon flakes easily with a fork.

5. Serve immediately, garnished with additional fresh dill and lemon slices if desired.

Nutritional Information per serving:
280 calories, 35g protein, 2g carbohydrates, 13g total fat, 0g fiber, 0mg cholesterol, 70mg sodium, 830mg potassium, 0g sugars.

2. Garden Fresh Grilled Vegetable Quinoa Salad

Yield: 4 servings | **Prep time:** 15 minutes | **Cook time:** 20 minutes

Ingredients:

- 1 cup quinoa
- 2 cups water
- 1 medium zucchini, sliced
- 2 bell peppers (one red, one yellow), seeded and sliced
- 1 cup cherry tomatoes, halved
- For the lemon vinaigrette:
  - Juice of 1 lemon
  - 3 tablespoons olive oil
  - 1 teaspoon honey
  - Salt and pepper to taste

Directions:

1. Rinse the quinoa under cold water. In a medium saucepan, bring 2 cups of water to a boil. Add the quinoa, reduce the heat to low, cover, and cook for 15 minutes, or until the water is absorbed. Fluff with a fork and let cool.

2. Preheat the grill to medium-high heat. Lightly brush the zucchini and bell peppers with olive oil and season with salt and pepper. Grill the vegetables, turning occasionally, until they are charred and tender, about 10 minutes. Remove from the grill and let cool slightly.

3. In a small bowl, whisk together the lemon juice, olive oil, honey, salt, and pepper to make the lemon vinaigrette. Adjust seasoning to taste.

4. In a large bowl, combine the cooked quinoa, grilled vegetables, and cherry tomatoes. Drizzle the lemon vinaigrette over the salad and toss to combine.

5. Serve the salad at room temperature or chilled, garnished with fresh herbs if desired.

Nutritional Information per serving:
220 calories, 8g protein, 34g carbohydrates, 7g total fat, 8g fiber, 0mg cholesterol, 85mg sodium, 480mg potassium, 6g sugars.

3. Hearty Stuffed Bell Peppers with Turkey and Brown Rice

Yield: 4 servings | **Prep time:** 20 minutes | **Cook time:** 45 minutes

Ingredients:

- 4 large bell peppers, any color
- 1 cup cooked brown rice
- 1 lb ground turkey
- 1 can (14.5 oz) diced tomatoes, drained
- 1 medium onion, finely chopped
- 2 cloves garlic, minced
- 1 teaspoon olive oil
- Salt and pepper to taste
- Optional: shredded cheese, fresh herbs for garnish

Directions:

1. Preheat your oven to 375°F (190°C). Slice the tops off the bell peppers and remove the seeds and membranes. Blanch the peppers in boiling water for 5 minutes to soften slightly, then drain and set aside.

2. In a skillet over medium heat, heat the olive oil and sauté the onion and garlic until translucent. Add the ground turkey and cook until browned. Season with salt and pepper.

3. Stir in the cooked brown rice and diced tomatoes. Cook for an additional 5 minutes, allowing the flavors to blend.

4. Stuff each bell pepper with the turkey and rice mixture. Place the stuffed peppers in a baking dish, and add a little water to the bottom of the dish to prevent sticking.

5. Cover with foil and bake in the preheated oven for 30 minutes. If desired, remove the foil, top with shredded cheese, and bake for an additional 10-15 minutes until the cheese is melted and bubbly.

6. Serve hot, garnished with fresh herbs if desired.

Nutritional Information per serving:
300 calories, 20g protein, 37g carbohydrates, 9g total fat, 5g fiber, 0mg cholesterol, 220mg sodium, 600mg potassium, 7g sugars.

4. Rustic Spinach and Mushroom Whole Wheat Pasta

Yield: 4 servings | **Prep time:** 10 minutes | **Cook time: 20 minutes**

Ingredients:

- 8 oz whole wheat pasta
- 2 cups fresh spinach
- 1 cup sliced mushrooms
- 2 tablespoons olive oil
- 2 cloves garlic, minced
- Salt and pepper to taste

Directions:

1. Cook the whole wheat pasta according to the package instructions until al dente. Drain and set aside, reserving a cup of pasta water.

2. While the pasta cooks, heat the olive oil in a large skillet over medium heat. Add the minced garlic and sliced mushrooms, sautéing until the mushrooms are soft and golden, about 5-7 minutes.

3. Add the fresh spinach to the skillet, stirring until the spinach wilts, about 2-3 minutes. If the mixture seems dry, add a little of the reserved pasta water to help deglaze the pan and create a light sauce.

4. Toss the cooked pasta with the spinach and mushroom mixture. Season with salt and pepper to taste. If needed, add more pasta water to achieve the desired sauce consistency.

5. Serve immediately, offering a nourishing and flavorful meal that combines the whole-grain goodness of whole wheat pasta with the nutritional benefits of spinach and mushrooms.

Nutritional Information per serving:
310 calories, 12g protein, 52g carbohydrates, 7g total fat, 10g fiber, 0mg cholesterol, 90mg sodium, 420mg potassium, 4g sugars.

5. Savory Heart-Healthy Chicken Stir-Fry

Yield: 4 servings | **Prep time:** 15 minutes |
Cook time: 20 minutes

Ingredients:
- 1 pound chicken breast, thinly sliced
- 2 cups broccoli florets
- 1 bell pepper, sliced
- 2 tablespoons low-sodium soy sauce
- 1 tablespoon fresh ginger, grated
- 2 cloves garlic, minced
- 1 tablespoon olive oil

Directions:
1. Heat the olive oil in a large skillet or wok over medium-high heat. Add the minced garlic and grated ginger, sautéing for about 1 minute until fragrant.

2. Add the thinly sliced chicken breast to the skillet and cook for 5-7 minutes, or until the chicken is browned and cooked through. Remove the chicken from the skillet and set aside.

3. In the same skillet, add the broccoli florets and bell pepper slices. Stir-fry for about 5 minutes, or until the vegetables are just tender but still crisp.

4. Return the cooked chicken to the skillet with the vegetables. Pour in the low-sodium soy sauce and toss everything together to coat the chicken and vegetables in the sauce. Cook for an additional 2-3 minutes, allowing the flavors to meld together.

5. Serve immediately, offering a balanced meal that combines lean protein, vibrant vegetables, and flavorful seasonings.

Nutritional Information per serving:
250 calories, 28g protein, 20g carbohydrates, 6g total fat, 4g fiber, 0mg cholesterol, 150mg sodium, 650mg potassium, 8g sugars.

6. Creamy Chickpea and Spinach Curry

Yield: 4 servings | **Prep time:** 10 minutes |
Cook time: 20 minutes

Ingredients:
- 2 cans (15 oz each) chickpeas, drained and rinsed
- 4 cups fresh spinach
- 1 can (14 oz) coconut milk
- 2 tablespoons curry powder
- 1 can (14 oz) diced tomatoes, drained
- 1 tablespoon olive oil
- Salt to taste

Directions:
1. Heat the olive oil in a large skillet over medium heat. Add the curry powder and sauté for about 1 minute, or until fragrant.

2. Add the chickpeas and diced tomatoes to the skillet. Stir to combine and cook for 5 minutes.

3. Pour in the coconut milk and bring the mixture to a simmer. Reduce the heat to low and cook for 10 minutes, allowing the flavors to meld together.

4. Gradually add the spinach to the skillet, stirring until it wilts and becomes part of the curry.

5. Season with salt to taste. Serve the curry warm, ideally over cooked rice or with naan bread.

Nutritional Information per serving:
260 calories, 12g protein, 38g carbohydrates, 9g total fat, 10g fiber, 0mg cholesterol, 200mg sodium, 540mg potassium, 6g sugars.

7. Citrus-Herb Baked Tilapia with Asparagus

Yield: 4 servings | **Prep time:** 10 minutes | **Cook time:** 20 minutes

Ingredients:
- 4 tilapia fillets (about 6 oz each)
- 2 lemons, thinly sliced
- 2 tablespoons fresh dill, chopped
- 2 tablespoons olive oil
- 1 bunch asparagus, trimmed
- Salt and pepper to taste

Directions:

1. Preheat the oven to 400°F (200°C). Line a baking sheet with parchment paper or lightly grease it.

2. Arrange the asparagus on the baking sheet and drizzle with 1 tablespoon of olive oil. Season with salt and pepper. Toss to coat and spread into a single layer.

3. Place the tilapia fillets on top of the asparagus. Season both sides of the fillets with salt and pepper.

4. Place lemon slices on top of each fillet and sprinkle with the chopped dill. Drizzle the remaining olive oil over the top.

5. Bake in the preheated oven for 12-15 minutes, or until the tilapia is flaky and cooked through, and the asparagus is tender.

6. Serve immediately, garnishing with additional lemon slices and dill if desired.

Nutritional Information per serving:
200 calories, 34g protein, 5g carbohydrates, 5g total fat, 2g fiber, 0mg cholesterol, 85mg sodium, 500mg potassium, 3g sugars.

8. Hearty Lentil Stew with Sweet Potatoes

Yield: 4 servings | **Prep time:** 15 minutes | **Cook time:** 40 minutes

Ingredients:
- 1 cup lentils, rinsed
- 2 large sweet potatoes, peeled and cubed
- 2 carrots, peeled and diced
- 2 stalks celery, diced
- 4 cups low-sodium vegetable broth
- Salt and pepper to taste
- Optional: herbs like thyme or rosemary for added flavor

Directions:

1. In a large pot, combine the rinsed lentils, cubed sweet potatoes, diced carrots, and diced celery.

2. Pour the low-sodium vegetable broth over the vegetables and lentils, ensuring they are fully submerged. Add more water if necessary to cover the ingredients.

3. Bring the stew to a boil over high heat, then reduce the heat to low. Cover and simmer for about 30-40 minutes, or until the lentils and sweet potatoes are tender.

4. Season the stew with salt and pepper to taste. If desired, add herbs like thyme or rosemary for additional flavor.

5. Serve the stew hot, either as is or with a side of whole grain bread for a complete meal.

Nutritional Information per serving:
240 calories, 14g protein, 45g carbohydrates, 1g total fat, 15g fiber, 0mg cholesterol, 120mg sodium, 850mg potassium, 9g sugars.

9. Savory Walnut-Crusted Pork Chops with Steamed Green Beans

Yield: 4 servings | **Prep time:** 15 minutes | **Cook time:** 25 minutes

Ingredients:
- 4 pork chops, boneless (about 6 oz each)
- 1 cup walnuts, finely chopped
- 1 tablespoon fresh rosemary, minced
- 2 tablespoons olive oil
- 2 cups green beans, trimmed
- Salt and pepper to taste

Directions:

1. Preheat your oven to 375°F (190°C). Line a baking sheet with parchment paper.

2. In a shallow dish, combine the finely chopped walnuts and minced rosemary. Season the pork chops with salt and pepper. Brush each chop with olive oil, then press each side into the walnut mixture to coat thoroughly.

3. Place the coated pork chops on the prepared baking sheet. Bake in the preheated oven for about 20-25 minutes, or until the internal temperature reaches 145°F (63°C) and the walnut crust is golden brown.

4. While the pork chops are baking, steam the green beans until tender but still crisp, about 4-5 minutes.

5. Serve the walnut-crusted pork chops immediately, accompanied by the steamed green beans.

Nutritional Information per serving:
330 calories, 38g protein, 9g carbohydrates, 15g total fat, 3g fiber, 0mg cholesterol, 200mg sodium, 740mg potassium, 2g sugars.

10. Golden Cauliflower Steak with Garlicky Kale

Yield: 4 servings | **Prep time:** 10 minutes | **Cook time:** 25 minutes

Ingredients:
- 2 large heads of cauliflower
- 2 teaspoons turmeric
- 4 cloves garlic, minced
- 3 tablespoons olive oil
- 4 cups kale, de-stemmed and chopped
- Salt and pepper to taste

Directions:

1. Preheat the oven to 400°F (200°C). Line a baking sheet with parchment paper.

2. Cut each head of cauliflower into thick slices (about 1-inch thick) to form "steaks." You should get about 2 good steaks per head of cauliflower; use the remaining florets for another recipe or roast them alongside the steaks.

3. Mix 2 tablespoons olive oil with turmeric, half of the minced garlic, salt, and pepper. Brush this mixture over both sides of each cauliflower steak.

4. Place the cauliflower steaks on the prepared baking sheet. Roast in the preheated oven for about 20-25 minutes, or until tender and golden on the edges, flipping once halfway through cooking.

5. While the cauliflower is roasting, heat the remaining tablespoon of olive oil in a large skillet over medium heat. Add the remaining garlic and sauté until fragrant. Add the kale and cook, stirring occasionally, until the kale is wilted and tender. Season with salt and pepper to taste.

6. Serve the cauliflower steaks with a side of garlicky kale.

Nutritional Information per serving:
150 calories, 6g protein, 18g carbohydrates, 7g total fat, 7g fiber, 0mg cholesterol, 90mg sodium, 670mg potassium, 5g sugars.

11. Zesty Tofu and Vegetable Skewers

Yield: 4 servings | **Prep time:** 20 minutes (plus marinating time) | **Cook time:** 10 minutes

Ingredients:
- 1 block (14 oz) firm tofu, pressed and cubed
- 1 medium zucchini, cut into 1/2-inch slices
- 1 cup cherry tomatoes
- 1 large red onion, cut into chunks
- Juice of 1 lemon
- 3 tablespoons olive oil
- 1 tablespoon mixed herbs (such as oregano, thyme, and basil), chopped
- Salt and pepper to taste

Directions:

1. In a bowl, whisk together lemon juice, olive oil, mixed herbs, salt, and pepper to create the marinade.

2. Add the cubed tofu, zucchini slices, cherry tomatoes, and red onion chunks to the marinade. Gently toss to coat. Cover and let marinate in the refrigerator for at least 30 minutes, or up to 2 hours for more flavor.

3. Preheat the grill to medium-high heat. Thread the marinated tofu and vegetables alternately onto skewers.

4. Grill the skewers for about 10 minutes, turning occasionally, until the vegetables are tender and the tofu is slightly charred.

5. Serve the skewers hot, with extra lemon wedges on the side for additional zest if desired.

Nutritional Information per serving:
180 calories, 12g protein, 15g carbohydrates, 8g total fat, 4g fiber, 0mg cholesterol, 60mg sodium, 300mg potassium, 4g sugars.

12. Garlic Roasted Chicken and Vegetables

Yield: 4 servings | **Prep time:** 15 minutes | **Cook time:** 35 minutes

Ingredients:
- 4 chicken breasts (boneless, skinless)
- 2 cups Brussels sprouts, halved
- 2 medium sweet potatoes, peeled and cubed
- 4 cloves garlic, minced
- 2 tablespoons fresh thyme leaves
- 3 tablespoons olive oil
- Salt and pepper to taste

Directions:

1. Preheat your oven to 425°F (220°C). Line a large baking sheet with parchment paper.

2. In a large bowl, combine the Brussels sprouts, sweet potatoes, minced garlic, and thyme. Drizzle with olive oil, season with salt and pepper, and toss to coat evenly.

3. Spread the vegetable mixture in a single layer on the prepared baking sheet. Nestle the chicken breasts among the vegetables.

4. Roast in the preheated oven for about 35 minutes, or until the chicken is cooked through (reaching an internal temperature of 165°F or 74°C) and the vegetables are tender and caramelized.

5. Serve hot, ensuring each plate gets a generous helping of both chicken and roasted vegetables.

Nutritional Information per serving:
310 calories, 35g protein, 25g carbohydrates, 9g total fat, 6g fiber, 0mg cholesterol, 210mg sodium, 800mg potassium, 7g sugars.

13. Vibrant Mediterranean Lentil Salad

Yield: 4 servings | **Prep time:** 15 minutes | **Cook time:** 20 minutes

Ingredients:

- 1 cup lentils, rinsed and drained
- 1 cucumber, diced
- 1 large tomato, diced
- 1/2 cup feta cheese, crumbled
- 1/2 cup olives, sliced
- 1/4 cup red onion, finely chopped
- For the lemon vinaigrette:
    - Juice of 1 lemon
    - 3 tablespoons olive oil
    - 1 garlic clove, minced
    - Salt and pepper to taste

Directions:

1. Cook the lentils in a large pot of boiling water according to package instructions until tender but firm, about 20 minutes. Drain and rinse under cold water to cool.

2. In a large bowl, combine the cooked lentils, diced cucumber, tomato, crumbled feta, sliced olives, and chopped red onion.

3. To make the lemon vinaigrette, whisk together lemon juice, olive oil, minced garlic, salt, and pepper in a small bowl until well combined.

4. Pour the vinaigrette over the salad and toss to coat all the ingredients evenly.

5. Chill the salad in the refrigerator for at least 30 minutes before serving to allow the flavors to meld.

Nutritional Information per serving:
250 calories, 17g protein, 35g carbohydrates, 6g total fat, 15g fiber, 0mg cholesterol, 180mg sodium, 400mg potassium, 5g sugars.

14. Light and Flavorful Baked Cod with Tomato and Basil

Yield: 4 servings | **Prep time:** 10 minutes | **Cook time:** 15 minutes

Ingredients:

- 4 cod fillets (6 oz each)
- 1 cup cherry tomatoes, halved
- 1/4 cup fresh basil leaves, chopped
- 2 cloves garlic, minced
- 2 tablespoons olive oil
- Salt and pepper to taste

Directions:

1. Preheat your oven to 400°F (200°C). Line a baking sheet with parchment paper or lightly grease it.

2. Arrange the cod fillets on the prepared baking sheet. Season both sides of each fillet with salt and pepper.

3. In a small bowl, mix together the cherry tomatoes, chopped basil, minced garlic, and olive oil. Season with a pinch of salt and pepper.

4. Spoon the tomato and basil mixture evenly over the top of each cod fillet.

5. Bake in the preheated oven for about 12-15 minutes, or until the fish flakes easily with a fork.

6. Serve immediately, garnished with additional fresh basil if desired.

Nutritional Information per serving:
200 calories, 34g protein, 6g carbohydrates, 4g total fat, 1g fiber, 0mg cholesterol, 70mg sodium, 500mg potassium, 3g sugars.

15. Veggie-Loaded Turkey Meatballs

Yield: 4 servings | **Prep time:** 15 minutes |
Cook time: 20 minutes

Ingredients:
- 1 pound ground turkey
- 1 cup grated zucchini, excess moisture removed
- 1/2 cup grated carrot
- 3/4 cup oats
- 2 cloves garlic, minced
- 1 large egg
- Salt and pepper, to taste

Directions:

1. Preheat the oven to 400°F (200°C). Line a baking sheet with parchment paper.

2. In a large bowl, mix together the ground turkey, grated zucchini, grated carrot, oats, minced garlic, and egg. Season with salt and pepper.

3. Shape the mixture into meatballs and place them on the prepared baking sheet.

4. Bake in the preheated oven for about 20 minutes, or until the meatballs are cooked through and slightly golden on the outside.

5. Serve hot, with your choice of sides or sauce.

Nutritional Information per serving:
220 calories, 26g protein, 12g carbohydrates, 8g total fat, 3g fiber, 95g cholesterol, 190mg sodium, 340mg potassium, 3g sugars.

16. Slow Cooker Moroccan Chicken Delight

Yield: 4 servings | **Prep time:** 15 minutes |
Cook time: 4 hours on high or 8 hours on low

Ingredients:
- 8 chicken thighs, skinless and boneless
- 1 can (15 oz) chickpeas, drained and rinsed
- 1 cup dried apricots, chopped
- 2 large tomatoes, diced
- 2 teaspoons Moroccan spices (ras el hanout or a blend of cumin, coriander, cinnamon, and ginger)
- 1 cup couscous
- Salt and pepper to taste
- 2 cups water or chicken broth (for the couscous)

Directions:

1. Season the chicken thighs with salt, pepper, and Moroccan spices. Place them in the slow cooker.

2. Add the chickpeas, dried apricots, and diced tomatoes over the chicken. Stir gently to mix the spices.

3. Cover and cook on high for 4 hours or on low for 8 hours, until the chicken is tender and fully cooked.

4. About 20 minutes before serving, prepare the couscous according to package instructions using water or chicken broth for added flavor.

5. Once the chicken is done, adjust seasoning if necessary. Serve the Moroccan chicken hot over a bed of fluffy couscous.

Nutritional Information per serving:
350 calories, 30g protein, 40g carbohydrates, 10g total fat, 8g fiber, 85 g cholesterol, 240mg sodium, 600mg potassium, 10g sugars.

17. Grilled Asparagus and Shrimp Quinoa Bowl

Yield: 4 servings | **Prep time:** 15 minutes | **Cook time:** 20 minutes

Ingredients:
- 1 cup quinoa, rinsed
- 2 cups water or vegetable broth
- 1 pound shrimp, peeled and deveined
- 1 bunch asparagus, trimmed and cut into 2-inch pieces
- Zest of 1 lemon
- 1/4 cup fresh parsley, chopped
- 2 tablespoons olive oil
- Salt and pepper to taste

Directions:
1. In a medium saucepan, bring the quinoa and water (or vegetable broth) to a boil. Reduce heat to low, cover, and simmer for 15 minutes, or until all liquid is absorbed. Remove from heat and let stand covered for 5 minutes. Fluff with a fork.

2. Preheat the grill to medium-high heat. Toss the shrimp and asparagus with 1 tablespoon olive oil, salt, and pepper. Grill the shrimp and asparagus for 2-3 minutes per side, or until the shrimp is opaque and the asparagus is tender and slightly charred.

3. In a large bowl, combine the cooked quinoa, grilled shrimp, and asparagus. Add the lemon zest, fresh parsley, and remaining tablespoon of olive oil. Toss to combine and season with additional salt and pepper if needed.

4. Serve immediately, divided into bowls.

Nutritional Information per serving:
280 calories, 20g protein, 32g carbohydrates, 8g total fat, 6g fiber, 120 g cholesterol, 200mg sodium, 480mg potassium, 3g sugars.

18. Hearty Vegetable and Barley Soup

Yield: 4 servings | **Prep time:** 15 minutes | **Cook time:** 30 minutes

Ingredients:
- 1/2 cup barley, rinsed
- 2 carrots, peeled and diced
- 2 stalks celery, diced
- 1 can (14.5 oz) diced tomatoes, undrained
- 2 cups spinach, roughly chopped
- 4 cups low-sodium vegetable broth

Directions:
1. In a large pot, bring the vegetable broth to a boil. Add the barley and reduce the heat to a simmer. Cover and cook for 10 minutes.

2. Add the diced carrots and celery to the pot. Continue to simmer, covered, for another 10 minutes, or until the vegetables start to soften.

3. Stir in the diced tomatoes (with their juice) and continue to simmer for another 5 minutes.

4. Add the spinach and cook for an additional 5 minutes, or until the spinach has wilted and the barley is tender.

5. Adjust the seasoning with salt and pepper to taste. Serve hot.

Nutritional Information per serving:
180 calories, 6g protein, 35g carbohydrates, 1g total fat, 9g fiber, 0mg cholesterol, 100mg sodium, 350mg potassium, 4g sugars.

19. Stuffed Acorn Squash with Quinoa and Cranberries

Yield: 4 servings | **Prep time:** 15 minutes | **Cook time:** 45 minutes

Ingredients:
- 2 acorn squash, halved and seeds removed
- 1 cup quinoa, rinsed
- 2 cups water
- 1/2 cup dried cranberries
- 1/2 cup walnuts, chopped
- 2 tablespoons fresh sage, chopped
- 2 tablespoons olive oil
- Salt and pepper to taste

Directions:
1. Preheat your oven to 400°F (200°C). Brush the inside and edges of the acorn squash halves with olive oil and season with salt and pepper. Place squash halves cut-side down on a baking sheet and roast for about 25-30 minutes, or until tender.

2. While the squash is roasting, combine the quinoa and water in a medium saucepan. Bring to a boil, then cover, reduce heat to low, and simmer for 15 minutes, or until all water is absorbed. Remove from heat and let sit, covered, for 5 minutes. Fluff with a fork.

3. Stir the dried cranberries, walnuts, and sage into the cooked quinoa. Season with salt and pepper to taste.

4. Once the squash halves are cooked and slightly cooled, fill them with the quinoa mixture.

5. Return the stuffed squash to the oven and bake for another 10-15 minutes, until the tops are slightly golden.

6. Serve warm, drizzled with a little more olive oil if desired.

Nutritional Information per serving:
300 calories, 6g protein, 50g carbohydrates, 8g total fat, 8g fiber, 0mg cholesterol, 85mg sodium, 780mg potassium, 12g sugars.

20. Seared Tuna Steak Salad

Yield: 4 servings | **Prep time:** 10 minutes | **Cook time:** 6 minutes

Ingredients:
- 4 tuna steaks (about 6 oz each)
- 8 cups mixed greens
- 1 ripe avocado, sliced
- 1 cup cherry tomatoes, halved
- 4 tablespoons balsamic glaze

Directions:
1. Heat a grill pan or skillet over high heat. Lightly brush the tuna steaks with olive oil and season with salt and pepper. Sear the tuna for about 2-3 minutes per side for medium-rare (adjust time if you prefer more or less done).

2. Arrange the mixed greens on plates. Top with sliced avocado and halved cherry tomatoes.

3. Slice the seared tuna steaks thinly and arrange on top of the salads.

4. Drizzle each salad with balsamic glaze just before serving.

Nutritional Information per serving:
290 calories, 35g protein, 20g carbohydrates, 9g total fat, 7g fiber, 60 g cholesterol, 180mg sodium, 510mg potassium, 6g sugars.

21. Eggplant and Chickpea Curry

Yield: 4 servings | **Prep time:** 15 minutes | **Cook time:** 30 minutes

Ingredients:
- 1 large eggplant, cut into cubes
- 1 can (15 oz) chickpeas, drained and rinsed
- 1 can (13.5 oz) coconut milk
- 2 tablespoons curry powder
- 2 tomatoes, diced
- 1/4 cup cilantro, chopped
- Salt to taste
- Olive oil for cooking

Directions:

1. Heat a large skillet over medium heat and add a drizzle of olive oil. Add the eggplant cubes and sauté until they start to soften, about 5 minutes.

2. Stir in the curry powder and cook for another minute until fragrant.

3. Add the chickpeas, diced tomatoes, and coconut milk to the skillet. Stir well to combine.

4. Bring the mixture to a simmer, then reduce the heat and continue to cook for about 20 minutes, or until the eggplant is tender and the sauce has thickened slightly.

5. Season with salt to taste. Just before serving, stir in the chopped cilantro.

6. Serve hot, ideally over a bed of rice or with naan bread.

Nutritional Information per serving:
240 calories, 9g protein, 35g carbohydrates, 8g total fat, 10g fiber, 0mg cholesterol, 220mg sodium, 560mg potassium, 8g sugars.

22. Spicy Black Bean and Corn Tacos

Yield: 4 servings | **Prep time:** 10 minutes | **Cook time:** 15 minutes

Ingredients:
- 1 can (15 oz) black beans, drained and rinsed
- 1 cup corn kernels (fresh or frozen and thawed)
- 4 whole wheat tortillas
- 1 ripe avocado, sliced
- Juice of 1 lime
- 1/4 cup fresh cilantro, chopped
- Salt and pepper to taste
- Optional: chili powder or cayenne pepper for extra spice

Directions:

1. In a skillet over medium heat, combine the black beans and corn. Cook for 5-7 minutes, or until thoroughly heated. Season with salt, pepper, and optional chili powder or cayenne pepper for added spice.

2. Warm the whole wheat tortillas in a separate skillet or in the microwave for about 30 seconds to make them pliable.

3. To assemble the tacos, distribute the black bean and corn mixture evenly among the tortillas.

4. Top each taco with avocado slices and a sprinkle of lime juice.

5. Garnish with fresh cilantro before serving.

Nutritional Information per serving:
260 calories, 10g protein, 42g carbohydrates, 7g total fat, 8g fiber, 0mg cholesterol, 200mg sodium, 380mg potassium, 5g sugars.

23. Lemon Pepper Trout with Wild Rice

Yield: 4 servings | **Prep time:** 20 minutes | **Cook time:** 30 minutes

Ingredients:
- 4 trout fillets
- 2 tablespoons lemon pepper seasoning
- 1 cup wild rice
- 1/4 cup chopped parsley
- 4 lemon wedges for serving

Directions:

1. Cook the wild rice according to package instructions until it's fluffy and all water is absorbed. Set aside and keep warm.

2. While the rice is cooking, season the trout fillets evenly with lemon pepper seasoning on both sides.

3. Heat a non-stick skillet over medium heat. Add the trout fillets skin-side down and cook for 4-5 minutes, then flip and cook for another 3-4 minutes or until the fish is cooked through and flakes easily with a fork.

4. Divide the cooked wild rice among plates. Place a trout fillet on top of each serving of rice.

5. Garnish each plate with chopped parsley and a lemon wedge. Serve immediately.

Nutritional Information per serving:
310 calories, 31g protein, 38g carbohydrates, 5g total fat, 4g fiber, 85 g cholesterol, 85mg sodium, 720mg potassium, 1g sugars.

24. Roasted Chickpea and Cauliflower Tacos

Yield: 4 servings | **Prep time:** 15 minutes | **Cook time:** 25 minutes

Ingredients:
- 1 can (15 oz) chickpeas, drained and rinsed
- 2 cups cauliflower florets
- 4 whole wheat tortillas
- Avocado cream (blend avocado with lime juice, salt, and a dash of water)
- Cabbage slaw (shredded cabbage mixed with a light vinaigrette)

Directions:

1. Preheat your oven to 400°F (200°C). Line a baking sheet with parchment paper.

2. Spread the chickpeas and cauliflower florets on the baking sheet. Drizzle with olive oil and season with your choice of spices (e.g., cumin, chili powder, garlic powder). Toss to coat evenly and roast in the oven for about 20-25 minutes, or until golden brown and crispy.

3. Warm the whole wheat tortillas in the oven for the last few minutes of roasting or on a skillet for about 30 seconds on each side.

4. To assemble the tacos, spread a layer of avocado cream on each tortilla, add a serving of the roasted chickpea and cauliflower mixture, and top with cabbage slaw.

5. Serve immediately with additional avocado cream and lime wedges on the side.

Nutritional Information per serving:
270 calories, 12g protein, 40g carbohydrates, 9g total fat, 12g fiber, 0 g cholesterol, 210mg sodium, 470mg potassium, 6g sugars.

25. Kale and White Bean Stuffed Portobello

Yield: 4 servings | **Prep time:** 20 minutes | **Cook time:** 20 minutes

Ingredients:
- 4 large Portobello mushroom caps
- 2 cups kale, chopped
- 1 can (15 oz) white beans, drained and rinsed
- 2 cloves garlic, minced
- 1/2 cup shredded mozzarella cheese

Directions:

1. Preheat the oven to 375°F (190°C). Clean the Portobello mushroom caps and remove the stems. Place them gill-side up on a baking sheet lined with parchment paper.

2. In a skillet over medium heat, sauté the garlic until fragrant, about 1 minute. Add the kale and sauté until it starts to wilt, about 3-4 minutes. Mix in the white beans and cook until heated through, about 2 minutes. Season with salt and pepper to taste.

3. Divide the kale and white bean mixture evenly among the mushroom caps. Sprinkle shredded mozzarella on top of each stuffed mushroom.

4. Bake in the preheated oven for about 15-20 minutes, or until the mushrooms are tender and the cheese is melted and slightly golden.

5. Serve warm, garnished with fresh herbs if desired.

Nutritional Information per serving:
180 calories, 15g protein, 25g carbohydrates, 4g total fat, 6g fiber, 22 g cholesterol, 125mg sodium, 670mg potassium, 2g sugars.

26. Ginger Soy Glazed Salmon

Yield: 4 servings | **Prep time:** 15 minutes | **Cook time:** 20 minutes

Ingredients:
- 4 salmon fillets
- 1/4 cup low sodium soy sauce
- 2 inches fresh ginger, grated
- 2 cloves garlic, minced
- 2 tablespoons honey

Directions:

1. In a bowl, whisk together the soy sauce, grated ginger, minced garlic, and honey to create the glaze.

2. Place the salmon fillets in a baking dish and pour the glaze over them, ensuring each fillet is evenly coated. Allow to marinate for at least 30 minutes in the refrigerator.

3. Preheat your oven to 400°F (200°C). Remove the salmon from the refrigerator and let it sit at room temperature for about 10 minutes.

4. Bake the salmon in the preheated oven for 15-20 minutes, or until the salmon is cooked through and flakes easily with a fork.

5. Optionally, you can broil the salmon for the last 2 minutes for a more caramelized top.

Nutritional Information per serving:
320 calories, 36g protein, 12g carbohydrates, 14g total fat, 0g fiber, 95 g cholesterol, 280mg sodium, 860mg potassium, 8g sugars.

27. Warm Barley and Roasted Vegetable Salad

Yield: 4 servings | **Prep time:** 15 minutes | **Cook time:** 30 minutes

Ingredients:
- 1 cup barley
- 2 bell peppers, chopped
- 1 zucchini, chopped
- 2 red onions, chopped
- 2 tablespoons olive oil
- 2 tablespoons balsamic vinegar

Directions:

1. Preheat the oven to 425°F (220°C). Toss the bell peppers, zucchini, and red onions with olive oil, and spread them on a baking sheet. Roast for about 20 minutes or until the vegetables are tender and slightly charred, stirring halfway through.

2. While the vegetables are roasting, cook the barley according to the package instructions until it's tender. Drain any excess water.

3. In a large bowl, combine the cooked barley with the roasted vegetables. Drizzle with balsamic vinegar and toss to coat everything evenly.

4. Serve the salad warm, optionally garnished with fresh herbs or a sprinkle of feta cheese for added flavor.

Nutritional Information per serving:
250 calories, 6g protein, 42g carbohydrates, 7g total fat, 9g fiber, 0g cholesterol, 90mg sodium, 400mg potassium, 5g sugars.

28. Lemon Herb Chicken Sheet Pan Dinner

Yield: 4 servings | **Prep time:** 10 minutes | **Cook time:** 25 minutes

Ingredients:
- 4 chicken breasts
- 1 bunch of asparagus, trimmed
- 1 cup cherry tomatoes
- 2 lemons, one sliced and one juiced
- 1 tablespoon each of fresh thyme and rosemary, chopped
- 2 tablespoons olive oil
- Salt and pepper to taste

Directions:

1. Preheat the oven to 400°F (200°C). In a large bowl, toss the chicken breasts, asparagus, and cherry tomatoes with olive oil, lemon juice, herbs, salt, and pepper until everything is well-coated.

2. Arrange the chicken and vegetables in a single layer on a large baking sheet. Place lemon slices over the chicken and vegetables for added flavor.

3. Bake in the preheated oven for about 25 minutes, or until the chicken is thoroughly cooked and the vegetables are tender and slightly charred.

4. Serve immediately, garnishing with additional fresh herbs if desired.

Nutritional Information per serving:
260 calories, 31g protein, 15g carbohydrates, 9g total fat, 4g fiber, 75 cholesterol, 190mg sodium, 550mg potassium, 4g sugars.

29. Spaghetti Squash with Tomato Basil Sauce

Yield: 4 servings | **Prep time:** 15 minutes | **Cook time:** 45 minutes

Ingredients:
- 1 large spaghetti squash
- 2 cups tomatoes, diced
- 3 cloves garlic, minced
- 1/4 cup fresh basil, chopped
- 2 tablespoons olive oil
- 1/4 cup grated Parmesan cheese
- Salt and pepper to taste

Directions:

1. Preheat the oven to 400°F (200°C). Halve the spaghetti squash lengthwise and scoop out the seeds. Place the squash halves cut-side down on a baking sheet and bake for 30-40 minutes, or until the flesh is easily pierced with a fork.

2. While the squash is baking, heat the olive oil in a pan over medium heat. Add the garlic and sauté for 1-2 minutes until fragrant. Add the tomatoes and cook for 5-10 minutes, until the tomatoes are soft and the sauce has thickened slightly. Stir in the basil and season with salt and pepper.

3. Once the squash is done, use a fork to scrape out the "spaghetti" strands into a bowl. Divide the spaghetti squash among plates, top with the tomato basil sauce, and sprinkle with grated Parmesan cheese.

4. Serve immediately, offering extra Parmesan cheese and fresh basil on the side if desired.

Nutritional Information per serving:
180 calories, 5g protein, 30g carbohydrates, 5g total fat, 6g fiber, 5 g cholesterol, 210mg sodium, 300mg potassium, 7g sugars.

30. Pesto Grilled Shrimp with Summer Squash

Yield: 4 servings | **Prep time:** 20 minutes | **Cook time:** 10 minutes

Ingredients:
- 1 lb shrimp, peeled and deveined
- 1/4 cup homemade or low-sodium pesto sauce
- 2 zucchinis, sliced
- 2 summer squashes, sliced
- 1 tablespoon olive oil
- Salt and pepper to taste

Directions:

1. Preheat the grill to medium-high heat. In a bowl, toss the shrimp with the pesto sauce until evenly coated. Let marinate for 10 minutes.

2. Thread the shrimp onto skewers, alternating with slices of zucchini and summer squash. Lightly brush the vegetables with olive oil and season with salt and pepper.

3. Grill the skewers for 2-3 minutes on each side, or until the shrimp are pink and opaque and the vegetables are tender.

4. Remove from the grill and serve immediately, with additional pesto sauce on the side if desired.

Nutritional Information per serving:
290 calories, 35g protein, 12g carbohydrates, 12g total fat, 3g fiber, 220 g cholesterol, 220mg sodium, 480mg potassium, 3g sugars.

Snacks and Smoothies: Quick Heart-Healthy Boosts

1. Avocado Lime Smoothie

Yield: 2 servings | **Prep time:** 5 minutes | **Cook time:** 0 minutes

Ingredients:

- 1/2 ripe avocado
- Juice of 1 lime
- 1 cup unsweetened almond milk
- 1 tablespoon honey
- Ice cubes

Directions:

1. Scoop out the avocado flesh and place it in a blender.
2. Add the lime juice, almond milk, and honey to the blender.
3. Add a cup of ice cubes to the mixture.
4. Blend on high until smooth and creamy.
5. Serve immediately in chilled glasses.

Nutritional Information per serving:
200 calories, 3g protein, 22g carbohydrates, 12g total fat, 7g fiber, 0mg cholesterol, 80mg sodium, 487mg potassium, 8g sugars.

2. Heart-Healthy Trail Mix

Yield: 4 servings | **Prep time:** 5 minutes | **Cook time:** 0 minutes

Ingredients:

- 1/4 cup almonds
- 1/4 cup walnuts
- 1/4 cup dried cranberries (no sugar added)
- 1/4 cup pumpkin seeds

Directions:

1. In a medium bowl, combine almonds, walnuts, dried cranberries, and pumpkin seeds.
2. Stir the mixture until the ingredients are well mixed.
3. Portion the mix into 1/4 cup servings for easy snack-sized packs.
4. Store the trail mix in an airtight container to maintain freshness.

Nutritional Information per serving:
210 calories, 7g protein, 18g carbohydrates, 15g total fat, 4g fiber, 0mg cholesterol, 50mg sodium, 260mg potassium, 7g sugars.

3. Banana Oat Energy Bars

Yield: 6 servings | **Prep time:** 15 minutes | **Cook time:** 20 minutes

Ingredients:

- 2 ripe bananas
- 1 cup rolled oats
- 1/4 cup almond butter
- 1/4 cup chopped walnuts
- 1 teaspoon cinnamon

Directions:

1. Preheat the oven to 350°F (175°C) and line a baking tray with parchment paper.

2. In a large bowl, mash the bananas until smooth. Mix in the rolled oats, almond butter, chopped walnuts, and cinnamon until well combined.

3. Spread the mixture evenly on the prepared baking tray, forming a rectangle about 1/2 inch thick.

4. Bake in the preheated oven for 18-20 minutes or until the edges are golden brown.

5. Allow to cool completely before cutting into bars.

Nutritional Information per serving:
190 calories, 5g protein, 27g carbohydrates, 8g total fat, 4g fiber, 0mg cholesterol, 10mg sodium, 330mg potassium, 9g sugars.

4. Kale Pineapple Smoothie

Yield: 2 servings | **Prep time:** 5 minutes | **Cook time:** 0 minutes

Ingredients:

- 1 cup chopped kale
- 1/2 cup frozen pineapple
- 1/2 banana
- 1 cup unsweetened almond milk

Directions:

1. Add the chopped kale, frozen pineapple, banana, and unsweetened almond milk to a blender.

2. Blend on high speed until smooth and creamy, scraping down the sides as necessary.

3. Pour into glasses and serve immediately.

Nutritional Information per serving:
180 calories, 4g protein, 35g carbohydrates, 3g total fat, 5g fiber, 0mg cholesterol, 85mg sodium, 420mg potassium, 14g sugars.

5. Cucumber Hummus Bites

Yield: 6 servings | **Prep time:** 10 minutes |
Cook time: 0 minutes

Ingredients:

- 1 large cucumber, sliced
- 1 cup hummus
- Paprika for garnish

Directions:

1. Slice the cucumber into 1/4 inch thick rounds.

2. Spoon about a teaspoon of hummus onto each cucumber slice.

3. Sprinkle a dash of paprika over each hummus-topped cucumber slice for garnish.

4. Arrange the cucumber bites on a serving platter and serve immediately.

Nutritional Information per serving:
150 calories, 7g protein, 14g carbohydrates, 9g total fat, 5g fiber, 0mg cholesterol, 120mg sodium, 220mg potassium, 2g sugars.

6. Ginger Berry Smoothie

Yield: 2 servings | **Prep time:** 5 minutes |
Cook time: 0 minutes

Ingredients:

- 1/2 cup blueberries
- 1/2 cup strawberries
- 1/2 inch fresh ginger, peeled and grated
- 1 cup unsweetened almond milk
- 1 tablespoon chia seeds

Directions:

1. Combine blueberries, strawberries, grated ginger, almond milk, and chia seeds in a blender.

2. Blend on high speed until smooth and creamy.

3. Pour the smoothie into glasses and serve immediately.

Nutritional Information per serving:
160 calories, 5g protein, 28g carbohydrates, 4g total fat, 8g fiber, 0mg cholesterol, 60mg sodium, 250mg potassium, 10g sugars.

7. Chickpea Salad Stuffed Mini Peppers

Yield: 4 servings | **Prep time:** 15 minutes | **Cook time:** 0 minutes

Ingredients:

- 1 cup cooked chickpeas
- 1/4 cup diced red onion
- 1/4 cup chopped parsley
- Juice of 1 lemon
- 8 mini bell peppers, halved and deseeded

Directions:

1. In a mixing bowl, combine the cooked chickpeas, diced red onion, chopped parsley, and lemon juice. Stir to mix well.

2. Carefully spoon the chickpea mixture into the halved mini bell peppers.

3. Serve immediately or refrigerate until ready to serve.

Nutritional Information per serving:
140 calories, 7g protein, 24g carbohydrates, 2g total fat, 7g fiber, 0mg cholesterol, 80mg sodium, 320mg potassium, 6g sugars.

8. Spinach and Berry Protein Smoothie

Yield: 2 servings | **Prep time:** 5 minutes | **Cook time:** 0 minutes

Ingredients:

- 1 cup fresh spinach
- 1/2 cup mixed berries (frozen)
- 1/2 banana
- 1 scoop whey protein powder (unsweetened, low sodium)
- 1 cup unsweetened almond milk

Directions:

1. In a blender, combine the spinach, mixed berries, banana, whey protein powder, and almond milk.

2. Blend on high speed until smooth and creamy.

3. Pour into glasses and serve immediately.

Nutritional Information per serving:
220 calories, 20g protein, 30g carbohydrates, 3g total fat, 6g fiber, 0mg cholesterol, 95mg sodium, 500mg potassium, 12g sugars.

9. Spicy Roasted Chickpeas

Yield: 2 servings | **Prep time:** 5 minutes |
Cook time: 20 minutes

Ingredients:

- 1 cup cooked chickpeas
- 1 teaspoon olive oil
- 1/4 teaspoon cayenne pepper
- 1/4 teaspoon garlic powder

Directions:

1. Preheat the oven to 400°F (200°C).
2. Rinse and drain the chickpeas, then pat dry with paper towels.
3. In a bowl, toss the chickpeas with olive oil, cayenne pepper, and garlic powder until evenly coated.
4. Spread the chickpeas on a baking sheet in a single layer.
5. Roast in the oven for 20 minutes, or until crispy, stirring halfway through.

Nutritional Information per serving:
150 calories, 7g protein, 22g carbohydrates, 4g total fat, 6g fiber, 0mg cholesterol, 120mg sodium, 210mg potassium, 3g sugars.

10. Almond Butter and Banana Slices on Whole Grain Toast

Yield: 1 serving | **Prep time:** 5 minutes |
Cook time: 0 minutes

Ingredients:

- 1 slice whole grain bread
- 1 tablespoon almond butter
- 1/2 sliced banana

Directions:

1. Toast the whole grain bread to your desired crispness.
2. Spread the almond butter evenly over the toasted bread.
3. Top the almond butter with banana slices.

Nutritional Information per serving:
200 calories, 6g protein, 28g carbohydrates, 8g total fat, 5g fiber, 0mg cholesterol, 120mg sodium, 350mg potassium, 10g sugars.

11. Avocado & Tomato Crispbreads

Yield: 1 serving | **Prep time:** 5 minutes | **Cook time:** 0 minutes

Ingredients:

- 2 whole grain crispbreads
- 1/2 ripe avocado, sliced
- 5 cherry tomatoes, halved
- Pinch of black pepper

Directions:

1. Lay the crispbreads on a flat surface.
2. Evenly distribute the sliced avocado over the crispbreads.
3. Place the halved cherry tomatoes on top of the avocado.
4. Season with a pinch of black pepper.

Nutritional Information per serving:
180 calories, 4g protein, 20g carbohydrates, 9g total fat, 6g fiber, 0mg cholesterol, 80mg sodium, 400mg potassium, 3g sugars.

12. Cool Cucumber Melon Smoothie

Yield: 2 servings | **Prep time:** 10 minutes | **Cook time:** 0 minutes

Ingredients:

- 1 cup honeydew melon chunks
- 1/2 cucumber, peeled and sliced
- 1/2 cup unsweetened Greek yogurt
- Mint leaves for garnish

Directions:

1. Combine honeydew melon, cucumber, and Greek yogurt in a blender.
2. Blend until smooth.
3. Pour the smoothie into glasses.
4. Garnish with mint leaves before serving.

Nutritional Information per serving:
100 calories, 7g protein, 18g carbohydrates, 0.5g total fat, 1g fiber, 0mg cholesterol, 35mg sodium, 420mg potassium, 12g sugars.

13. Heart-Healthy Trail Mix

Yield: 4 servings | **Prep time:** 10 minutes | **Cook time:** 0 minutes

Ingredients:

- 1/4 cup walnuts
- 1/4 cup almonds
- 1/4 cup dried cranberries (unsweetened)
- 1/4 cup dark chocolate chips (at least 70% cocoa)

Directions:

1. Combine walnuts, almonds, dried cranberries, and dark chocolate chips in a large bowl.
2. Stir the mixture to ensure even distribution of ingredients.
3. Divide the mixture into individual serving containers or bags.
4. Store in a cool, dry place to maintain freshness.

Nutritional Information per serving:
200 calories, 5g protein, 18g carbohydrates, 14g total fat, 3g fiber, 0mg cholesterol, 10mg sodium, 220mg potassium, 8g sugars.

14. Green Tea and Berry Fusion Smoothie

Yield: 2 servings | **Prep time:** 5 minutes | **Cook time:** 0 minutes

Ingredients:

- 1/2 cup brewed green tea (cooled)
- 1/2 cup mixed berries (frozen)
- 1/2 banana
- 1/2 cup spinach
- 1 tablespoon flaxseeds

Directions:

1. Brew the green tea and allow it to cool, or use pre-cooled tea.
2. In a blender, combine the cooled green tea, frozen mixed berries, banana, spinach, and flaxseeds.
3. Blend until smooth and creamy, adjusting the consistency with more tea or water if needed.
4. Pour into glasses and serve immediately, garnished with a few whole berries or a mint leaf if desired.

Nutritional Information per serving:
120 calories, 3g protein, 22g carbohydrates, 2g total fat, 5g fiber, 0mg cholesterol, 20mg sodium, 300mg potassium, 9g sugars.

15. Sweet Potato Hummus Dip

Yield: 4 servings | **Prep time:** 10 minutes | **Cook time:** 0 minutes (assuming the sweet potato is already cooked)

Ingredients:

- 1 small sweet potato (cooked and mashed)
- 1 cup chickpeas
- 1 tablespoon tahini
- 1 garlic clove, minced
- Lemon juice (to taste)
- Cumin (to taste)

Directions:

1. In a blender or food processor, combine the cooked and mashed sweet potato, chickpeas, tahini, minced garlic, a squeeze of lemon juice, and a sprinkle of cumin.

2. Blend until smooth and creamy, scraping down the sides as needed to ensure even mixing.

3. Taste and adjust the seasoning, adding more lemon juice, cumin, or a pinch of salt if necessary.

4. Transfer the hummus to a serving bowl and chill in the refrigerator for at least 30 minutes to allow the flavors to meld.

5. Serve with a drizzle of olive oil on top and a sprinkle of paprika, if desired, alongside fresh vegetables or whole-grain crackers for dipping.

Nutritional Information per serving:
150 calories, 5g protein, 24g carbohydrates, 4g total fat, 6g fiber, 0mg cholesterol, 120mg sodium, 480mg potassium, 3g sugars.

16. Chilled Avocado Soup Shots

Yield: 4 servings | **Prep time:** 10 minutes | **Cook time:** 0 minutes (chill time not included)

Ingredients:

- 1 ripe avocado
- 1/2 cucumber, peeled and chopped
- 1 cup low-sodium vegetable broth
- Lime juice (to taste)
- Cilantro (to garnish)

Directions:

1. Scoop out the avocado flesh and place it in a blender along with the chopped cucumber and vegetable broth.

2. Blend until the mixture is smooth and creamy.

3. Add lime juice to taste and blend again to mix well.

4. Pour the soup into shot glasses or small serving cups and refrigerate until chilled, about 30 minutes to 1 hour.

5. Garnish with cilantro before serving.

Nutritional Information per serving:
90 calories, 2g protein, 8g carbohydrates, 7g total fat, 4g fiber, 0mg cholesterol, 55mg sodium, 350mg potassium, 2g sugars.

17. Berry Quinoa Salad Cups

Yield: 4 servings | **Prep time:** 10 minutes | **Cook time:** 0 minutes

Ingredients:

- 1/2 cup cooked quinoa (cooled)
- 1/4 cup blueberries
- 1/4 cup sliced strawberries
- 1 tablespoon chopped nuts
- Lemon zest (to taste)
- A drizzle of honey

Directions:

1. In a bowl, combine the cooled quinoa with blueberries and sliced strawberries.
2. Add the chopped nuts and mix gently to combine.
3. Zest a lemon over the salad for a fresh flavor boost and drizzle with honey to sweeten.
4. Spoon the mixture into individual serving cups or small bowls.
5. Chill in the refrigerator for a few minutes before serving to allow the flavors to meld.

Nutritional Information per serving:
120 calories, 4g protein, 21g carbohydrates, 3g total fat, 3g fiber, 0mg cholesterol, 10mg sodium, 220mg potassium, 6g sugars.

18. Peachy Keen Smoothie

Yield: 2 servings | **Prep time:** 5 minutes | **Cook time:** 0 minutes

Ingredients:

- 1 ripe peach, sliced
- 1/2 banana
- 1/2 cup almond milk
- 1/2 teaspoon vanilla extract
- A pinch of cinnamon

Directions:

1. Place the sliced peach and banana in a blender.
2. Add almond milk and vanilla extract.
3. Sprinkle a pinch of cinnamon for added flavor.
4. Blend until smooth and creamy.
5. Pour into glasses and serve immediately for a refreshing treat.

Nutritional Information per serving:
150 calories, 2g protein, 35g carbohydrates, 1.5g total fat, 4g fiber, 0mg cholesterol, 80mg sodium, 450mg potassium, 18g sugars.

19. Almond Butter & Banana Rice Cakes

Yield: 2 servings | **Prep time:** 5 minutes |
Cook time: 0 minutes

Ingredients:

- 2 brown rice cakes
- 1 tablespoon almond butter
- 1 small banana, sliced
- A sprinkle of chia seeds

Directions:

1. Spread 1/2 tablespoon of almond butter evenly on each rice cake.
2. Place sliced banana on top of the almond butter on each rice cake.
3. Sprinkle chia seeds over the banana slices for added texture and nutrients.
4. Serve immediately and enjoy as a nutritious snack or light meal.

Nutritional Information per serving:
210 calories, 5g protein, 32g carbohydrates, 8g total fat, 5g fiber, 0mg cholesterol, 60mg sodium, 400mg potassium, 10g sugars.

20. Spinach and Pineapple Energizer Smoothie

Yield: 2 servings| **Prep time:** 5 minutes |
Cook time: 0 minutes

Ingredients:

- 1 cup fresh spinach
- 1/2 cup frozen pineapple chunks
- 1/2 banana
- 1/2 cup coconut water
- 1 tablespoon chia seeds

Directions:

1. Add the fresh spinach, frozen pineapple chunks, and banana to a blender.
2. Pour in the coconut water and add the chia seeds.
3. Blend on high until smooth and creamy.
4. Pour the smoothie into glasses and serve immediately for a refreshing and energizing drink.

Nutritional Information per serving:
130 calories, 3g protein, 26g carbohydrates, 2g total fat, 5g fiber, 0mg cholesterol, 30mg sodium, 490mg potassium, 12g sugars.

Soups and Salads: Comfort in Every Spoonful and Crunch

1. Golden Turmeric Lentil Soup

Yield: 4 servings | **Prep time:** 10 minutes | **Cook time:** 25 minutes

Ingredients:

- 1 cup red lentils
- 2 carrots, diced
- 2 celery stalks, diced
- 1 teaspoon turmeric
- 2 garlic cloves, minced
- 4 cups low-sodium vegetable broth
- 2 cups spinach leaves

Directions:

1. Rinse the lentils under cold water until the water runs clear.

2. In a large pot, sauté the carrots, celery, and garlic until softened, about 5 minutes.

3. Stir in the turmeric and lentils, then add the vegetable broth. Bring to a boil.

4. Reduce heat and simmer for 20 minutes, or until lentils are tender.

5. Add the spinach and cook until wilted, about 2 minutes. Adjust seasoning to taste.

6. Serve hot for a comforting and nutritious meal.

Nutritional Information per serving:
220 calories, 14g protein, 40g carbohydrates, 1g total fat, 15g fiber, 0mg cholesterol, 120mg sodium, 600mg potassium, 4g sugars.

2. Avocado and Grapefruit Salad

Yield: 4 servings | **Prep time:** 15 minutes | **Cook time:** 0 minutes

Ingredients:

- 4 cups mixed greens
- 1 avocado, peeled, pitted, and sliced
- 1 grapefruit, peeled and segmented
- 1/2 cup walnuts, chopped
- 2 tablespoons olive oil
- 1 tablespoon white wine vinegar

Directions:

1. In a large salad bowl, combine mixed greens, avocado slices, and grapefruit segments.

2. In a small bowl, whisk together olive oil and white wine vinegar to make the dressing.

3. Drizzle the dressing over the salad and gently toss to combine.

4. Sprinkle chopped walnuts on top of the salad.

5. Serve immediately for a refreshing and nutritious meal.

Nutritional Information per serving:
250 calories, 4g protein, 18g carbohydrates, 20g total fat, 7g fiber, 0mg cholesterol, 85mg sodium, 500mg potassium, 8g sugars.

3. Hearty Vegetable Barley Soup

Yield: 4 servings | **Prep time:** 15 minutes | **Cook time:** 45 minutes

Ingredients:

- 1/2 cup pearl barley
- 1 can (14.5 oz) diced tomatoes, undrained
- 1 zucchini, diced
- 4 cups low-sodium vegetable broth
- 2 cups chopped kale
- 1 teaspoon dried thyme

Directions:

1. Rinse the barley under cold water and drain.
2. In a large pot, combine the barley, diced tomatoes, and vegetable broth. Bring to a boil.
3. Reduce heat to low, cover, and simmer for 30 minutes.
4. Add the diced zucchini, kale, and thyme to the pot. Simmer for another 15 minutes or until the barley and vegetables are tender.
5. Adjust seasoning to taste and serve hot.

Nutritional Information per serving:
180 calories, 6g protein, 35g carbohydrates, 1g total fat, 9g fiber, 0mg cholesterol, 100mg sodium, 400mg potassium, 5g sugars.

4. Spinach and Strawberry Salad

Yield: 4 servings | **Prep time:** 10 minutes | **Cook time:** 0 minutes

Ingredients:

- 4 cups fresh spinach
- 1 cup sliced strawberries
- 1/4 cup almonds, sliced or chopped
- 1/2 cup goat cheese, crumbled
- Balsamic glaze for drizzling

Directions:

1. In a large bowl, combine the spinach and sliced strawberries.
2. Add the sliced almonds and crumbled goat cheese to the bowl.
3. Drizzle with balsamic glaze and gently toss to combine all ingredients.
4. Serve immediately, ensuring each serving has a good mix of all ingredients.

Nutritional Information per serving:
200 calories, 7g protein, 20g carbohydrates, 11g total fat, 4g fiber, 0mg cholesterol, 150mg sodium, 360mg potassium, 7g sugars.

5. Roasted Butternut Squash Soup

Yield: 4 servings | **Prep time:** 15 minutes | **Cook time:** 45 minutes

Ingredients:

- 1 large butternut squash, peeled, seeded, and cubed
- 4 cups low-sodium vegetable broth
- 1 medium onion, chopped
- 2 cloves garlic, minced
- 1/4 teaspoon nutmeg
- 1/4 teaspoon cinnamon
- 1 cup coconut milk

Directions:

1. Preheat the oven to 400°F (200°C). Place the butternut squash on a baking sheet, drizzle with olive oil, and roast for 25-30 minutes until tender.

2. In a large pot, sauté the onion and garlic until translucent. Add the roasted squash, nutmeg, and cinnamon, and cook for a few minutes.

3. Pour in the vegetable broth and bring to a simmer. Cook for 15 minutes.

4. Blend the soup using an immersion blender until smooth. Stir in the coconut milk and heat through.

5. Season with salt and pepper to taste and serve hot.

Nutritional Information per serving:
210 calories, 3g protein, 40g carbohydrates, 5g total fat, 6g fiber, 0mg cholesterol, 130mg sodium, 550mg potassium, 9g sugars.

6. Quinoa and Black Bean Salad

Yield: 4 servings | **Prep time:** 20 minutes | **Cook time:** 0 minutes (assuming quinoa and black beans are pre-cooked)

Ingredients:

- 1 cup cooked quinoa
- 1 cup black beans, rinsed and drained
- 1 cup corn (fresh, canned, or thawed from frozen)
- 1 red bell pepper, diced
- 1/4 cup chopped cilantro
- Lime vinaigrette: juice of 1 lime, 2 tablespoons olive oil, salt, and pepper to taste

Directions:

1. In a large bowl, combine the cooked quinoa, black beans, corn, and diced red bell pepper.

2. In a small bowl, whisk together the lime juice, olive oil, salt, and pepper to create the vinaigrette.

3. Pour the vinaigrette over the salad and toss to combine evenly.

4. Stir in the chopped cilantro and adjust seasoning if necessary.

5. Serve chilled or at room temperature.

Nutritional Information per serving:
240 calories, 11g protein, 42g carbohydrates, 5g total fat, 9g fiber, 0mg cholesterol, 85mg sodium, 480mg potassium, 3g sugars.

7. Creamy Carrot Ginger Soup

Yield: 4 servings | **Prep time:** 15 minutes | **Cook time:** 25 minutes

Ingredients:

- 1 lb carrots, peeled and chopped
- 2 inches fresh ginger, peeled and minced
- 1 large onion, chopped
- 4 cups low-sodium vegetable broth
- 1 cup coconut milk
- 2 tablespoons lemon juice
- Salt and pepper to taste

Directions:

1. In a large pot, sauté the onion and ginger until the onion is translucent, about 5 minutes.

2. Add the chopped carrots and vegetable broth, bring to a boil, then reduce heat and simmer until carrots are tender, about 20 minutes.

3. Puree the mixture in the pot using an immersion blender until smooth. Stir in coconut milk and lemon juice, then season with salt and pepper to taste.

4. Simmer for an additional 5 minutes, then remove from heat.

5. Serve hot, garnished with a swirl of coconut milk or fresh herbs if desired.

Nutritional Information per serving:
190 calories, 2g protein, 30g carbohydrates, 6g total fat, 5g fiber, 0mg cholesterol, 95mg sodium, 370mg potassium, 9g sugars.

8. Mediterranean Chickpea Salad

Yield: 4 servings | **Prep time:** 15 minutes | **Cook time:** 0 minutes (no cooking required)

Ingredients:

- 1 can (15 oz) chickpeas, drained and rinsed
- 1 cucumber, diced
- 1 cup cherry tomatoes, halved
- 1/2 cup olives, pitted and sliced
- 1/2 cup feta cheese, crumbled
- 1/4 cup red onion, finely chopped
- 1/4 cup lemon-herb dressing

Directions:

1. In a large bowl, combine chickpeas, cucumber, cherry tomatoes, olives, and red onion.

2. Drizzle the lemon-herb dressing over the salad and toss to combine.

3. Sprinkle feta cheese over the top and gently mix into the salad.

4. Let the salad sit for at least 10 minutes before serving to allow flavors to meld.

Nutritional Information per serving:
260 calories, 12g protein, 35g carbohydrates, 9g total fat, 10g fiber, 0mg cholesterol, 180mg sodium, 460mg potassium, 6g sugars.

9. Tomato Basil Soup

Yield: 4 servings | **Prep time:** 10 minutes | **Cook time:** 30 minutes

Ingredients:

- 1 can (28 oz) crushed tomatoes
- 2 cups low-sodium vegetable broth
- 1/4 cup fresh basil, chopped
- 2 cloves garlic, minced
- 1 medium onion, chopped
- 2 tablespoons olive oil

Directions:

1. In a large pot, heat the olive oil over medium heat. Add the chopped onion and minced garlic, sautéing until the onion is translucent.

2. Stir in the crushed tomatoes and vegetable broth, bringing the mixture to a simmer.

3. Reduce the heat to low and simmer for 20 minutes, allowing the flavors to meld.

4. Add the chopped basil, and continue to simmer for an additional 10 minutes.

5. Use an immersion blender to puree the soup until smooth (optional).

Nutritional Information per serving:
150 calories, 4g protein, 25g carbohydrates, 4g total fat, 6g fiber, 0mg cholesterol, 120mg sodium, 550mg potassium, 9g sugars.

10. Cucumber and Dill Salad

Yield: 4 servings | **Prep time:** 15 minutes | **Cook time:** 0 minutes

Ingredients:

- 2 large cucumbers, thinly sliced
- 2 tablespoons fresh dill, chopped
- 1/2 cup yogurt dressing
- 1/4 red onion, thinly sliced
- 2 tablespoons lemon juice
- 1 clove garlic, minced

Directions:

1. In a large bowl, combine the thinly sliced cucumbers, chopped dill, and thinly sliced red onion.

2. In a small bowl, whisk together the yogurt dressing, lemon juice, and minced garlic.

3. Pour the dressing over the cucumber mixture and toss to coat evenly.

4. Chill in the refrigerator for at least 30 minutes before serving to allow flavors to meld.

Nutritional Information per serving:
110 calories, 6g protein, 18g carbohydrates, 2g total fat, 2g fiber, 0mg cholesterol, 55mg sodium, 250mg potassium, 5g sugars.

11. Avocado and Grapefruit Salad

Yield: 4 servings | **Prep time:** 15 minutes | **Cook time:** 0 minutes

Ingredients:

- Mixed greens
- 1 avocado, sliced
- 1 grapefruit, segmented
- 1/4 cup walnut pieces
- Balsamic vinaigrette

Directions:

1. Arrange mixed greens on a serving platter or in a large salad bowl.

2. Top the greens with evenly distributed avocado slices and grapefruit segments.

3. Sprinkle walnut pieces over the salad.

4. Drizzle with balsamic vinaigrette just before serving.

Nutritional Information per serving:
230 calories, 4g protein, 21g carbohydrates, 15g total fat, 7g fiber, 0mg cholesterol, 85mg sodium, 490mg potassium, 8g sugars.

12. Lentil and Kale Soup

Yield: 4 servings | **Prep time:** 15 minutes | **Cook time:** 40 minutes

Ingredients:

- 1 cup lentils
- 2 cups kale, chopped
- 2 carrots, diced
- 1 onion, chopped
- 4 cups low-sodium vegetable broth
- 1 tsp thyme

Directions:

1. Rinse lentils and set aside. In a large pot, sauté onions and carrots until softened.

2. Add lentils, vegetable broth, and thyme to the pot. Bring to a boil, then reduce heat to simmer.

3. Cook until lentils are tender, about 30 minutes.

4. Stir in kale and cook until wilted, about 5 to 10 minutes. Adjust seasoning as needed.

Nutritional Information per serving:
210 calories, 14g protein, 38g carbohydrates, 1g total fat, 15g fiber, 0mg cholesterol, 90mg sodium, 610mg potassium, 4g sugars.

13. Roasted Beet and Goat Cheese Salad

Yield: 4 servings | **Prep time:** 15 minutes (excluding beet roasting time) |
Cook time: 45 minutes (for roasting beets)

Ingredients:

- Roasted beets (4 medium beets)
- 4 cups mixed greens
- 1/2 cup goat cheese, crumbled
- 1/4 cup walnuts, chopped
- Balsamic reduction for drizzling

Directions:

1. Preheat the oven to 400°F (200°C). Wrap beets in foil and roast until tender, about 45 minutes. Allow to cool, then peel and slice.

2. Arrange mixed greens on plates. Top with sliced roasted beets and crumbled goat cheese.

3. Sprinkle with chopped walnuts and drizzle with balsamic reduction.

4. Serve immediately, with extra balsamic reduction on the side if desired.

Nutritional Information per serving:
260 calories, 8g protein, 21g carbohydrates, 17g total fat, 5g fiber, 0mg cholesterol, 180mg sodium, 520mg potassium, 9g sugars.

14. Chicken Minestrone Soup

Yield: 4 servings | **Prep time:** 15 minutes |
Cook time: 30 minutes

Ingredients:

- 1 chicken breast, cooked and shredded
- 1 cup kidney beans, drained and rinsed
- 1 medium zucchini, diced
- 2 carrots, peeled and diced
- 4 cups low-sodium chicken broth
- 1 can (14.5 oz) diced tomatoes
- 1/2 cup pasta (e.g., elbow macaroni or small shells)

Directions:

1. In a large pot, combine chicken broth, diced tomatoes, carrots, and bring to a boil.

2. Add the pasta to the boiling broth and cook for about 10 minutes, or until halfway done.

3. Add the zucchini, kidney beans, and cooked chicken breast to the pot. Simmer until the vegetables are tender and the pasta is cooked, about 15-20 minutes.

4. Season the soup with salt and pepper to taste, and serve hot, garnished with fresh herbs if desired.

Nutritional Information per serving:
250 calories, 20g protein, 37g carbohydrates, 3g total fat, 8g fiber, 0mg cholesterol, 190mg sodium, 670mg potassium, 6g sugars.

15. Spinach and Strawberry Salad

Yield: 4 servings | **Prep time:** 15 minutes | **Cook time:** 0 minutes (no cooking required)

Ingredients:

- 4 cups baby spinach
- 2 cups strawberries, hulled and sliced
- 1/4 cup sliced almonds
- 1/2 cup feta cheese, crumbled
- 1/4 cup poppy seed dressing

Directions:

1. In a large salad bowl, combine the baby spinach and sliced strawberries.

2. Sprinkle the sliced almonds and crumbled feta cheese over the salad.

3. Drizzle the poppy seed dressing over the salad and gently toss to coat evenly.

4. Serve immediately for the freshest taste.

Nutritional Information per serving:
180 calories, 6g protein, 20g carbohydrates, 9g total fat, 4g fiber, 0mg cholesterol, 250mg sodium, 360mg potassium, 7g sugars.

16. Curried Butternut Squash Soup

Yield: 4 servings | **Prep time:** 15 minutes | **Cook time:** 30 minutes

Ingredients:

- 1 medium butternut squash, peeled, seeded, and cubed
- 4 cups low-sodium vegetable broth
- 1 large onion, chopped
- 2 cloves garlic, minced
- 2 teaspoons curry powder
- 1 cup coconut milk

Directions:

1. In a large pot, sauté onion and garlic until translucent.

2. Add the cubed butternut squash and curry powder, stirring to coat.

3. Pour in the vegetable broth and bring to a boil. Reduce heat and simmer until squash is tender.

4. Blend the soup using an immersion blender or in batches with a regular blender until smooth.

5. Stir in coconut milk and heat through. Adjust seasoning to taste.

Nutritional Information per serving:
190 calories, 3g protein, 34g carbohydrates, 5g total fat, 6g fiber, 0mg cholesterol, 150mg sodium, 480mg potassium, 8g sugars.

17. Quinoa Tabbouleh Salad

Yield: 4 servings | **Prep time:** 20 minutes | **Cook time:** 15 minutes

Ingredients:

- 1 cup quinoa, rinsed
- 1 cucumber, diced
- 2 tomatoes, diced
- 1 cup chopped parsley
- 1/4 cup chopped mint
- Juice of 1 lemon
- 2 tablespoons olive oil
- Salt and pepper to taste

Directions:

1. Cook quinoa according to package instructions and let it cool.

2. In a large bowl, combine the cooled quinoa, cucumber, tomatoes, parsley, and mint.

3. In a small bowl, whisk together lemon juice, olive oil, salt, and pepper.

4. Pour the dressing over the quinoa mixture and toss to combine.

5. Chill in the refrigerator before serving to allow flavors to meld.

Nutritional Information per serving:
220 calories, 6g protein, 30g carbohydrates, 9g total fat, 5g fiber, 0mg cholesterol, 30mg sodium, 370mg potassium, 3g sugars.

18. Tomato Basil Soup

Yield: 4 servings | **Prep time:** 10 minutes | **Cook time:** 30 minutes

Ingredients:

- 2 lbs fresh tomatoes, chopped
- 2 cups low-sodium vegetable broth
- 1 large onion, chopped
- 2 garlic cloves, minced
- 1/4 cup fresh basil leaves, chopped
- 2 tablespoons olive oil
- 1 tablespoon balsamic vinegar
- Salt and pepper to taste

Directions:

1. In a large pot, heat the olive oil over medium heat. Add the onion and garlic, sauté until softened, about 5 minutes.

2. Add the chopped tomatoes and cook for another 10 minutes, stirring occasionally.

3. Pour in the vegetable broth and bring the mixture to a boil. Reduce heat and simmer for 15 minutes.

4. Stir in the fresh basil and balsamic vinegar, and cook for an additional 5 minutes.

5. Use an immersion blender to puree the soup until smooth. Season with salt and pepper to taste.

6. Serve hot, garnished with extra basil leaves if desired.

Nutritional Information per serving:
120 calories, 2g protein, 16g carbohydrates, 5g total fat, 3g fiber, 0mg cholesterol, 70mg sodium, 410mg potassium, 6g sugars.

19. Cucumber Noodle Salad

Yield: 4 servings | **Prep time:** 15 minutes | **Cook time:** 0 minutes (no cooking required)

Ingredients:

- 2 large cucumbers, spiralized into noodles
- 1 cup cherry tomatoes, halved
- 1/2 cup olives, pitted and sliced
- 1/2 cup feta cheese, crumbled
- 1/4 cup red onion, thinly sliced
- 1/4 cup lemon vinaigrette

Directions:

1. In a large bowl, combine the cucumber noodles, cherry tomatoes, olives, and red onion.
2. Drizzle the lemon vinaigrette over the salad and toss gently to combine.
3. Sprinkle the feta cheese over the top of the salad just before serving.
4. Serve chilled, garnished with fresh herbs if desired.

Nutritional Information per serving:
160 calories, 4g protein, 18g carbohydrates, 7g total fat, 2g fiber, 0mg cholesterol, 180mg sodium, 270mg potassium, 4g sugars.

20. Sweet Potato and Lentil Soup

Yield: 4 servings | **Prep time:** 15 minutes | **Cook time:** 30 minutes

Ingredients:

- 2 medium sweet potatoes, peeled and cubed
- 1 cup dried lentils, rinsed
- 1 large carrot, diced
- 2 stalks celery, diced
- 4 cups low-sodium vegetable broth
- 2 cups fresh spinach, roughly chopped
- 1 teaspoon ground cumin
- 1 onion, diced
- 2 cloves garlic, minced
- Salt and pepper, to taste

Directions:

1. In a large pot, heat a drizzle of olive oil over medium heat. Add the diced onion and minced garlic, sautéing until they are translucent and fragrant, about 3-5 minutes.
2. Add the cubed sweet potatoes, diced carrot, and celery to the pot. Cook for another 5 minutes until slightly softened.
3. Stir in the rinsed lentils and pour in the vegetable broth. Bring the mixture to a boil, then reduce heat to simmer. Cover and cook for about 20-25 minutes, or until the lentils and vegetables are tender.
4. Add the chopped spinach and ground cumin to the soup. Stir well and continue to simmer for another 5 minutes, allowing the spinach to wilt and the flavors to meld.
5. Season with salt and pepper to taste. Serve hot.

Nutritional Information per serving:
240 calories, 12g protein, 47g carbohydrates, 1g total fat, 12g fiber, 0mg cholesterol, 130mg sodium, 650mg potassium, 7g sugars.

Side Dishes: Perfect Pairings for Any Meal

1. Hearty Heart-Healthy Coleslaw

Yield: 4 servings | **Prep time:** 15 minutes | **Cook time:** 0 minutes

Ingredients:

- 4 cups cabbage, shredded
- 2 medium carrots, shredded
- 2 tablespoons apple cider vinegar
- 1 tablespoon honey
- 2 tablespoons olive oil
- 1/4 teaspoon black pepper

Directions:

1. In a large bowl, combine the shredded cabbage and carrots.
2. In a small bowl, whisk together apple cider vinegar, honey, olive oil, and black pepper to create the dressing.
3. Pour the dressing over the cabbage and carrot mixture and toss well to coat evenly.
4. Let the coleslaw sit for at least 10 minutes before serving to allow flavors to meld.
5. Serve chilled or at room temperature.

Nutritional Information per serving:
70 calories, 1g protein, 10g carbohydrates, 3g total fat, 3g fiber, 0mg cholesterol, 20mg sodium, 150mg potassium, 4g sugars.

2. Savory Garlic Green Beans

Yield: 4 servings | **Prep time:** 10 minutes | **Cook time:** 10 minutes

Ingredients:

- 1 lb fresh green beans, ends trimmed
- 3 cloves garlic, minced
- 2 tablespoons olive oil
- 1 teaspoon lemon zest

Directions:

1. Heat olive oil in a large skillet over medium heat. Add the minced garlic and sauté for 1 minute until fragrant.
2. Add the green beans and cook, stirring occasionally, for 8-10 minutes, or until they are tender but still slightly crisp.
3. Remove from heat and stir in the lemon zest. Season with salt and pepper to taste.
4. Serve the green beans hot, garnished with additional lemon zest if desired.

Nutritional Information per serving:
60 calories, 2g protein, 9g carbohydrates, 2g total fat, 4g fiber, 0mg cholesterol, 10mg sodium, 200mg potassium, 2g sugars.

3. Mediterranean Quinoa Salad

Yield: 4 servings | **Prep time:** 15 minutes |
Cook time: 15 minutes

Ingredients:

- 1 cup quinoa, rinsed
- 2 cups water
- 1 cup cherry tomatoes, halved
- 1 cucumber, diced
- 1/2 cup olives, pitted and halved
- 2 tablespoons lemon juice
- 1/4 cup fresh parsley, chopped
- Salt and pepper, to taste

Directions:

1. In a medium saucepan, bring 2 cups of water to a boil. Add the quinoa, reduce heat to low, cover, and simmer for 15 minutes, or until the water is absorbed and the quinoa is tender.

2. Fluff the cooked quinoa with a fork and allow it to cool to room temperature.

3. In a large bowl, combine the cooled quinoa, cherry tomatoes, cucumber, and olives.

4. Drizzle with lemon juice, add chopped parsley, and season with salt and pepper to taste. Toss everything to combine well.

5. Chill the salad in the refrigerator for at least 30 minutes before serving to enhance the flavors.

Nutritional Information per serving:
120 calories, 4g protein, 18g carbohydrates, 4g total fat, 3g fiber, 0mg cholesterol, 30mg sodium, 220mg potassium, 3g sugars.

4. Roasted Turmeric Cauliflower

Yield: 4 servings | **Prep time:** 10 minutes |
Cook time: 25 minutes

Ingredients:

- 1 large head of cauliflower, cut into florets
- 2 teaspoons turmeric
- 2 tablespoons olive oil
- Pinch of salt

Directions:

1. Preheat the oven to 400°F (200°C).

2. In a large bowl, toss the cauliflower florets with olive oil, turmeric, and a pinch of salt until evenly coated.

3. Spread the cauliflower in a single layer on a baking sheet lined with parchment paper.

4. Roast in the preheated oven for 25 minutes, or until the cauliflower is tender and has golden brown edges, stirring halfway through the cooking time.

5. Remove from the oven and let cool slightly before serving.

Nutritional Information per serving:
80 calories, 3g protein, 10g carbohydrates, 4g total fat, 4g fiber, 0mg cholesterol, 30mg sodium, 320mg potassium, 3g sugars.

5. Heart-Friendly Beetroot Salad

Yield: 4 servings | **Prep time:** 15 minutes | **Cook time:** 0 minutes (assuming using pre-cooked beets)

Ingredients:

- 4 medium beets, cooked and sliced
- 4 cups arugula
- 1/2 cup walnuts, chopped
- 2 tablespoons balsamic vinegar
- 1/4 cup goat cheese, crumbled

Directions:

1. Arrange arugula leaves on a serving platter as the salad base.
2. Top the arugula with sliced beets, distributing them evenly.
3. Sprinkle chopped walnuts over the beets.
4. Drizzle balsamic vinegar evenly over the salad.
5. Garnish with crumbled goat cheese just before serving.

Nutritional Information per serving:
110 calories, 4g protein, 13g carbohydrates, 5g total fat, 3g fiber, 0mg cholesterol, 55mg sodium, 370mg potassium, 7g sugars.

6. Zesty Lemon Asparagus

Yield: 4 servings | **Prep time:** 10 minutes | **Cook time:** 10 minutes

Ingredients:

- 1 pound asparagus spears, trimmed
- 2 tablespoons lemon juice
- 1 tablespoon olive oil
- 1 teaspoon mixed herbs (such as thyme, oregano, or parsley)

Directions:

1. Preheat your oven to 400°F (200°C) or prepare a grill for medium heat.
2. Toss the asparagus spears with olive oil, lemon juice, and mixed herbs until evenly coated.
3. Lay the asparagus on a baking sheet in a single layer (for oven roasting) or place on the grill.
4. Roast or grill the asparagus for about 10 minutes, turning once, until they are tender and lightly charred.

Nutritional Information per serving:
50 calories, 3g protein, 6g carbohydrates, 2g total fat, 3g fiber, 0mg cholesterol, 20mg sodium, 230mg potassium, 2g sugars.

7. Sweet Potato Mash Bliss

Yield: 4 servings | **Prep time:** 15 minutes | **Cook time:** 20 minutes

Ingredients:

- 2 large sweet potatoes, peeled and cubed
- 1/2 teaspoon cinnamon
- 1/4 teaspoon nutmeg
- 1/2 cup almond milk

Directions:

1. Place the cubed sweet potatoes in a large pot of boiling water. Cook until tender, about 15-20 minutes.
2. Drain the sweet potatoes and return them to the pot.
3. Add cinnamon, nutmeg, and almond milk to the sweet potatoes.
4. Mash the mixture until smooth and well combined.

Nutritional Information per serving:
150 calories, 2g protein, 33g carbohydrates, 1g total fat, 5g fiber, 0mg cholesterol, 55mg sodium, 440mg potassium, 6g sugars.

8. Balsamic Brussels Sprouts

Yield: 4 servings | **Prep time:** 10 minutes | **Cook time:** 20 minutes

Ingredients:

- 1 pound Brussels sprouts, trimmed and halved
- 2 tablespoons olive oil
- 2 tablespoons balsamic vinegar
- 1/4 teaspoon black pepper

Directions:

1. Preheat the oven to 400°F (200°C).
2. In a large bowl, toss the Brussels sprouts with olive oil, balsamic vinegar, and black pepper.
3. Spread the Brussels sprouts on a baking sheet in a single layer.
4. Roast in the oven until caramelized and tender, about 20 minutes, stirring halfway through.

Nutritional Information per serving:
90 calories, 4g protein, 12g carbohydrates, 4g total fat, 4g fiber, 0mg cholesterol, 25mg sodium, 350mg potassium, 3g sugars.

9. Cucumber and Tomato Toss

Yield: 4 servings | **Prep time:** 15 minutes | **Cook time:** 0 minutes

Ingredients:

- 2 large cucumbers, peeled and diced
- 2 cups cherry tomatoes, halved
- 1/2 red onion, thinly sliced
- 2 tablespoons vinegar
- 2 tablespoons fresh dill, chopped

Directions:

1. In a large bowl, combine the cucumbers, cherry tomatoes, and red onion.
2. Drizzle with vinegar and toss to coat evenly.
3. Sprinkle with fresh dill and gently toss again.
4. Serve immediately or chill in the refrigerator for 30 minutes before serving to enhance the flavors.

Nutritional Information per serving:
50 calories, 2g protein, 10g carbohydrates, 0g total fat, 2g fiber, 0mg cholesterol, 10mg sodium, 220mg potassium, 4g sugars.

10. Ginger Stir-Fried Broccoli

Yield: 4 servings | **Prep time:** 10 minutes | **Cook time:** 10 minutes

Ingredients:

- 4 cups broccoli florets
- 1 tablespoon fresh ginger, minced
- 2 garlic cloves, minced
- 1 tablespoon sesame oil

Directions:

1. Heat sesame oil in a large skillet or wok over medium-high heat.
2. Add the minced ginger and garlic to the skillet and sauté for 1 minute until fragrant.
3. Add the broccoli florets and stir-fry for 8-10 minutes or until the broccoli is tender but still crisp.
4. Serve hot as a side dish or incorporate into a main meal.

Nutritional Information per serving:
70 calories, 3g protein, 9g carbohydrates, 3g total fat, 3g fiber, 0mg cholesterol, 30mg sodium, 290mg potassium, 2g sugars.

11. Spiced Carrot Ribbons

Yield: 4 servings | **Prep time:** 15 minutes | **Cook time:** 5 minutes

Ingredients:

- 4 large carrots, peeled into ribbons
- 1 teaspoon cumin
- 1 teaspoon paprika
- 1 tablespoon olive oil
- 2 tablespoons fresh parsley, chopped

Directions:

1. In a large bowl, combine carrot ribbons, cumin, paprika, and olive oil. Toss until the carrots are evenly coated with the spices and oil.

2. Heat a large pan over medium heat and add the spiced carrot ribbons. Sauté for 3-5 minutes until the carrots are tender yet slightly crisp.

3. Remove from heat, garnish with fresh parsley, and serve warm as a flavorful side dish.

Nutritional Information per serving:
60 calories, 1g protein, 10g carbohydrates, 2g total fat, 3g fiber, 0mg cholesterol, 40mg sodium, 270mg potassium, 5g sugars.

12. Eggplant Caponata Delight

Yield: 4 servings | **Prep time:** 15 minutes | **Cook time:** 30 minutes

Ingredients:

- 1 large eggplant, cut into 1/2-inch cubes
- 2 medium tomatoes, chopped
- 2 tablespoons capers, drained
- 3 tablespoons olive oil
- 2 tablespoons red wine vinegar

Directions:

1. Heat 2 tablespoons of olive oil in a large skillet over medium heat. Add the eggplant cubes and cook until they are golden and softened, about 10-12 minutes.

2. Add the chopped tomatoes and capers to the skillet. Cook for another 5 minutes, until the tomatoes soften and the mixture is well combined.

3. Stir in the red wine vinegar and cook for an additional 2 minutes. Remove from heat and let it cool to room temperature.

4. Drizzle with the remaining tablespoon of olive oil, toss gently, and serve either warm or at room temperature.

Nutritional Information per serving:
100 calories, 2g protein, 13g carbohydrates, 5g total fat, 5g fiber, 0mg cholesterol, 50mg sodium, 300mg potassium, 6g sugars.

13. Citrus Infused Artichokes

Yield: 4 servings | **Prep time:** 15 minutes | **Cook time:** 25 minutes

Ingredients:

- 4 large artichokes, trimmed and halved
- 1/4 cup lemon juice
- 2 tablespoons olive oil
- 2 garlic cloves, minced

Directions:

1. In a large pot, bring water to a boil and steam the artichokes until tender, about 20 minutes.

2. In a small bowl, whisk together lemon juice, olive oil, and minced garlic to create a marinade.

3. Once the artichokes are cooked and slightly cooled, brush them with the citrus marinade.

4. Preheat the grill or broiler. Grill or broil the artichokes for about 5 minutes, or until they are lightly charred and the flavors are infused.

Nutritional Information per serving:
90 calories, 4g protein, 12g carbohydrates, 4g total fat, 5g fiber, 0mg cholesterol, 60mg sodium, 370mg potassium, 1g sugars.

14. Kale and Apple Slaw

Yield: 4 servings | **Prep time:** 15 minutes | **Cook time:** 0 minutes

Ingredients:

- 4 cups chopped kale
- 1 large apple, cored and thinly sliced
- 1/4 cup lemon dressing
- 1/4 cup sliced almonds

Directions:

1. In a large bowl, combine the chopped kale and sliced apple.

2. Drizzle the lemon dressing over the kale and apple mixture, and toss to coat evenly.

3. Let the slaw sit for 10 minutes to allow the flavors to meld and the kale to soften.

4. Just before serving, sprinkle with sliced almonds and toss again.

Nutritional Information per serving:
100 calories, 3g protein, 13g carbohydrates, 5g total fat, 3g fiber, 0mg cholesterol, 25mg sodium, 320mg potassium, 6g sugars.

15. Roasted Garlic and Herb Mushrooms

Yield: 4 servings | **Prep time:** 10 minutes | **Cook time:** 20 minutes

Ingredients:

- 1 lb mushrooms, cleaned and halved
- 4 cloves garlic, minced
- 1 tbsp fresh thyme, chopped
- 2 tbsp olive oil
- Salt, to taste

Directions:

1. Preheat the oven to 400°F (200°C).
2. In a large bowl, toss the mushrooms with the minced garlic, thyme, olive oil, and a pinch of salt until well coated.
3. Spread the mushroom mixture in a single layer on a baking sheet.
4. Roast in the preheated oven for 20 minutes, or until the mushrooms are tender and golden brown.
5. Serve warm as a side dish or a topping for grilled meats or salads.

Nutritional Information per serving:

80 calories, 3g protein, 10g carbohydrates, 4g total fat, 3g fiber, 0mg cholesterol, 20mg sodium, 380mg potassium, 2g sugars.

16. Tangy Radish and Cucumber Salad

Yield: 4 servings | **Prep time:** 15 minutes | **Cook time:** 0 minutes

Ingredients:

- 1 cup radishes, thinly sliced
- 1 large cucumber, thinly sliced
- 1/2 cup yogurt dressing
- 2 tbsp lemon juice
- 1 tbsp chives, finely chopped

Directions:

1. In a large bowl, combine the thinly sliced radishes and cucumber.
2. In a small bowl, whisk together the yogurt dressing and lemon juice until smooth.
3. Pour the dressing over the radish and cucumber slices, tossing gently to coat.
4. Sprinkle with chopped chives and toss again lightly.
5. Chill in the refrigerator for about 10 minutes before serving to allow the flavors to meld.

Nutritional Information per serving:

60 calories, 3g protein, 10g carbohydrates, 1g total fat, 2g fiber, 0mg cholesterol, 30mg sodium, 250mg potassium, 3g sugars.

Heart-Healthy Desserts: Sweet Endings Without the Guilt

1. Berry Bliss Sorbet

Yield: 4 servings | **Prep time:** 10 minutes | **Cook time:** 0 minutes (plus freezing time)

Ingredients:

- 3 cups frozen mixed berries
- 2 tablespoons lemon juice
- 1/4 cup honey

Directions:

1. In a blender or food processor, combine the frozen mixed berries, lemon juice, and honey. Blend until smooth.

2. Taste the mixture and adjust sweetness if necessary by adding a little more honey.

3. Transfer the mixture to a freezer-safe container and freeze until firm, about 2-3 hours, stirring every 30 minutes to break up any large ice crystals.

4. Let the sorbet sit at room temperature for a few minutes before scooping and serving.

Nutritional Information per serving:
90 calories, 1g protein, 23g carbohydrates, 0g total fat, 3g fiber, 0mg cholesterol, 5mg sodium, 120mg potassium, 12g sugars.

2. Cinnamon Apple Crisps

Yield: 4 servings | **Prep time:** 10 minutes | **Cook time:** 15 minutes

Ingredients:

- 2 large apples, thinly sliced
- 1 teaspoon cinnamon
- 1 tablespoon honey

Directions:

1. Preheat your oven to 200°F (93°C) and line a baking sheet with parchment paper.

2. Arrange the apple slices in a single layer on the baking sheet.

3. Drizzle honey over the apple slices and sprinkle them with cinnamon.

4. Bake in the preheated oven for 15 minutes, then flip the slices and continue baking until crisp, about 1 hour more.

5. Let the apple crisps cool before serving to allow them to crisp up further.

Nutritional Information per serving:
60 calories, 0g protein, 16g carbohydrates, 0g total fat, 2g fiber, 0mg cholesterol, 2mg sodium, 95mg potassium, 11g sugars.

3. Chia Seed Pudding Delight

Yield: 4 servings | **Prep time:** 10 minutes (plus soaking time) | **Cook time:** 0 minutes

Ingredients:

- 1/4 cup chia seeds
- 2 cups unsweetened almond milk
- 1/2 teaspoon vanilla extract
- 1 cup fresh berries (such as strawberries, blueberries, or raspberries)

Directions:

1. In a mixing bowl, combine the chia seeds, almond milk, and vanilla extract. Whisk thoroughly to combine.

2. Cover the mixture and refrigerate for at least 4 hours, preferably overnight, allowing the chia seeds to absorb the liquid and form a pudding-like texture.

3. Stir the pudding once more before serving. If it's too thick, add a little more almond milk to reach the desired consistency.

4. Serve the chia pudding in bowls or glasses and top with fresh berries.

Nutritional Information per serving:
120 calories, 3g protein, 17g carbohydrates, 4g total fat, 5g fiber, 0mg cholesterol, 30mg sodium, 150mg potassium, 6g sugars.

4. Heart-Happy Almond Cookies

Yield: 6 servings | **Prep time:** 15 minutes | **Cook time:** 12 minutes

Ingredients:

- 1 cup ground almonds
- 1/2 cup whole wheat flour
- 1/4 cup olive oil
- 1/4 cup erythritol

Directions:

1. Preheat the oven to 350°F (175°C). Line a baking sheet with parchment paper.

2. In a bowl, mix ground almonds, whole wheat flour, and erythritol.

3. Gradually add olive oil to the dry ingredients, stirring until the mixture forms a dough.

4. Shape the dough into small balls and place them on the prepared baking sheet. Flatten each ball slightly with your fingers or the back of a spoon.

5. Bake in the preheated oven for 10-12 minutes or until the edges are golden brown.

6. Remove from the oven and let cool on the baking sheet for 5 minutes, then transfer to a wire rack to cool completely.

Nutritional Information per serving:
100 calories, 3g protein, 9g carbohydrates, 6g total fat, 2g fiber, 0mg cholesterol, 20mg sodium, 75mg potassium, 2g sugars.

5. Avocado Chocolate Mousse

Yield: 4 servings | **Prep time:** 10 minutes | **Cook time:** 0 minutes (chill time in the fridge for at least 30 minutes before serving)

Ingredients:

- 2 ripe avocados
- 1/4 cup cocoa powder
- 1/4 cup maple syrup
- 1 teaspoon vanilla extract

Directions:

1. Scoop out the avocado flesh and place it in a food processor or blender.
2. Add cocoa powder, maple syrup, and vanilla extract to the avocado.
3. Blend until the mixture is smooth and creamy, scraping down the sides as necessary.
4. Divide the mousse into serving dishes and refrigerate for at least 30 minutes to set.
5. Serve chilled as a decadent dessert.

Nutritional Information per serving:
150 calories, 2g protein, 17g carbohydrates, 10g total fat, 6g fiber, 0mg cholesterol, 10mg sodium, 360mg potassium, 8g sugars.

6. Peachy Keen Compote

Yield: 4 servings | **Prep time:** 10 minutes | **Cook time:** 15 minutes

Ingredients:

- 4 fresh peaches, pitted and sliced
- Zest of 1 lemon
- 1 tablespoon honey
- 1/2 teaspoon cinnamon

Directions:

1. In a saucepan over medium heat, combine the sliced peaches, lemon zest, honey, and cinnamon.
2. Cook, stirring occasionally, until the peaches are soft and the mixture has thickened, about 15 minutes.
3. Remove from heat and let cool slightly. The compote will thicken further as it cools.
4. Serve warm or chill in the refrigerator before serving.

Nutritional Information per serving:
70 calories, 1g protein, 18g carbohydrates, 0g total fat, 2g fiber, 0mg cholesterol, 0mg sodium, 190mg potassium, 15g sugars.

7. Ginger Pear Bake

Yield: 4 servings | **Prep time:** 10 minutes | **Cook time:** 25 minutes

Ingredients:

- 4 large pears, cored and sliced
- 1 teaspoon fresh ginger, grated
- 1/4 teaspoon nutmeg
- 1/4 cup almond milk

Directions:

1. Preheat the oven to 350°F (175°C).
2. In a mixing bowl, combine the sliced pears, grated ginger, and nutmeg.
3. Pour the mixture into a baking dish and drizzle with almond milk.
4. Bake in the preheated oven for 25 minutes, or until the pears are tender and lightly browned.
5. Serve warm.

Nutritional Information per serving:
80 calories, 1g protein, 20g carbohydrates, 0.5g total fat, 4g fiber, 0mg cholesterol, 5mg sodium, 125mg potassium, 12g sugars.

8. Coconut Water Fruit Jelly

Yield: 4 servings | **Prep time:** 15 minutes | **Cook time:** 5 minutes (plus chilling time)

Ingredients:

- 2 cups coconut water
- 2 teaspoons agar agar powder
- 2 cups mixed fruit (such as berries, diced mango, and kiwi)
- 1 tablespoon honey

Directions:

1. In a small saucepan, combine the coconut water and agar agar. Let sit for 5 minutes to soften.
2. Heat the mixture over medium heat, stirring until the agar agar is completely dissolved. Add honey and stir until well combined.
3. Arrange the mixed fruit in serving dishes or a mold.
4. Pour the warm coconut water mixture over the fruit. Refrigerate until set, about 2 hours.
5. Serve chilled as a refreshing dessert.

Nutritional Information per serving:
50 calories, 0g protein, 12g carbohydrates, 0g total fat, 2g fiber, 0mg cholesterol, 30mg sodium, 100mg potassium, 9g sugars.

9. No-Guilt Berry Crumble

Yield: 4 servings | **Prep time:** 10 minutes | **Cook time:** 30 minutes

Ingredients:

- 2 cups mixed berries (fresh or frozen)
- 1 cup rolled oats
- 1/2 cup almond meal
- 1/2 cup unsweetened apple sauce

Directions:

1. Preheat the oven to 375°F (190°C).
2. In a baking dish, evenly spread the mixed berries.
3. In a bowl, combine the rolled oats, almond meal, and apple sauce until the mixture is well combined and crumbly.
4. Sprinkle the oat mixture over the berries in the baking dish.
5. Bake in the preheated oven for 30 minutes, or until the topping is golden brown and the berries are bubbling.
6. Let cool slightly before serving.

Nutritional Information per serving:
130 calories, 2g protein, 24g carbohydrates, 3g total fat, 4g fiber, 0mg cholesterol, 15mg sodium, 115mg potassium, 9g sugars.

10. Tropical Mango Freeze

Yield: 4 servings | **Prep time:** 10 minutes | **Cook time:** 0 minutes (freeze time may vary)

Ingredients:

- 2 cups frozen mango chunks
- Juice of 1 lime
- 1/2 cup coconut milk
- 1 tablespoon honey

Directions:

1. In a blender, combine the frozen mango chunks, lime juice, coconut milk, and honey.
2. Blend until smooth and creamy.
3. Pour the mixture into a container and freeze until firm, about 2-4 hours, stirring occasionally.
4. Scoop and serve chilled.

Nutritional Information per serving:
100 calories, 1g protein, 20g carbohydrates, 2g total fat, 3g fiber, 0mg cholesterol, 10mg sodium, 180mg potassium, 16g sugars.

11. Banana Nut Soft Serve

Yield: 4 servings | **Prep time:** 5 minutes | **Cook time:** 0 minutes (plus freezing time for bananas)

Ingredients:

- 4 large bananas, peeled, sliced, and frozen
- 1/2 cup walnuts
- 1/2 teaspoon cinnamon
- 1/4 teaspoon nutmeg

Directions:

1. Freeze sliced bananas until solid, at least 2 hours or overnight.
2. Place the frozen banana slices in a food processor or high-powered blender.
3. Add the walnuts, cinnamon, and nutmeg to the bananas.
4. Blend until smooth and creamy, scraping down the sides as necessary.
5. Serve immediately for a soft-serve consistency, or freeze for an additional hour for a firmer texture.

Nutritional Information per serving:
110 calories, 2g protein, 18g carbohydrates, 4g total fat, 3g fiber, 0mg cholesterol, 0mg sodium, 320mg potassium, 14g sugars.

12. Zesty Lemon Raspberry Cups

Yield: 4 servings | **Prep time:** 10 minutes | **Cook time:** 0 minutes

Ingredients:

- 2 cups fresh raspberries
- Juice of 1 lemon
- 2 cups Greek yogurt
- 2 tablespoons honey

Directions:

1. In a bowl, combine the Greek yogurt and honey. Stir until well mixed.
2. Squeeze the lemon juice over the raspberries and gently toss to coat.
3. Layer the Greek yogurt mixture and lemon-tossed raspberries in serving cups.
4. Garnish with a few whole raspberries and a sprinkle of lemon zest if desired.
5. Serve immediately or chill in the refrigerator until ready to serve.

Nutritional Information per serving:
90 calories, 5g protein, 16g carbohydrates, 1g total fat, 4g fiber, 0mg cholesterol, 15mg sodium, 110mg potassium, 8g sugars.

13. Chocolate Avocado Truffles

Yield: 4 servings | **Prep time:** 15 minutes | **Cook time:** 0 minutes (chill time 30 minutes)

Ingredients:

- 1 ripe avocado
- 4 ounces dark chocolate (70% cocoa)
- 2 tablespoons cocoa powder for coating
- A dash of sea salt

Directions:

1. Melt the dark chocolate in a heatproof bowl over a pot of simmering water or in the microwave in short bursts, stirring until smooth.

2. Mash the avocado in a bowl until very smooth with no lumps. Mix the melted chocolate and a dash of sea salt into the mashed avocado until well combined.

3. Chill the mixture in the refrigerator for about 20-30 minutes or until it's firm enough to handle.

4. Using a spoon, scoop out the mixture and roll into balls. Then roll each ball in cocoa powder to coat.

5. Place the truffles on a baking sheet lined with parchment paper and refrigerate until set, about 10 minutes.

Nutritional Information per serving:
100 calories, 2g protein, 9g carbohydrates, 7g total fat, 3g fiber, 0mg cholesterol, 25mg sodium, 200mg potassium, 5g sugars.

14. Spiced Orange Segments

Yield: 4 servings | **Prep time:** 10 minutes | **Cook time:** 0 minutes

Ingredients:

- 4 large oranges, segmented
- 1/2 teaspoon cinnamon
- 1/4 teaspoon cardamom
- 1 tablespoon honey

Directions:

1. Peel the oranges and segment them, removing any seeds and pith.

2. In a mixing bowl, combine the orange segments with cinnamon and cardamom.

3. Drizzle honey over the spiced oranges and gently toss to combine.

4. Let the mixture sit for 5 minutes to allow the flavors to meld before serving.

Nutritional Information per serving:
60 calories, 1g protein, 15g carbohydrates, 0g total fat, 3g fiber, 0mg cholesterol, 0mg sodium, 180mg potassium, 12g sugars.

Chapter 4: Lifestyle Beyond the Kitchen: Exercise and Stress Management

Living with congestive heart failure (CHF) presents unique challenges, but it also opens up opportunities to embrace lifestyle adjustments that can profoundly impact well-being. As we delve into this chapter, we aim to equip you with knowledge, strategies, and inspiration to incorporate regular physical activity and effective stress management techniques into your daily life. Together, these elements form a triad of health—alongside nutrition—that can significantly improve your quality of life, enhance cardiac function, and promote longevity.

The Importance of Physical Activity

Understanding Exercise and CHF: A Foundation for Healing and Strength

The journey of managing Congestive Heart Failure (CHF) is unique for every individual, yet a universal cornerstone of this journey is the incorporation of regular physical activity. Understanding the profound impact exercise can have on the cardiovascular system, particularly for those with CHF, is the first step towards embracing a more active lifestyle that can significantly enhance heart health and overall well-being.

Physiological Benefits of Exercise on the Cardiovascular System

- **Enhancing Heart Efficiency:**
  Exercise acts as a catalyst for improving the heart's efficiency. For individuals with CHF, the heart struggles to pump blood efficiently, leading to a cascade of symptoms that can affect every aspect of life. Engaging in regular, moderate exercise has been shown to strengthen the heart muscle. This strengthening allows the heart to pump blood more effectively, reducing the workload required to circulate blood throughout the body. Over time, this increased efficiency can lead to a decrease in CHF symptoms, such as shortness of breath and fatigue, making daily activities more manageable.

- **Improving Circulation and Reducing Blood Pressure:**
  Physical activity helps to improve circulation and lower blood pressure, two factors that are vital in managing CHF. As exercise stimulates blood flow, it encourages the widening of blood vessels, a process known as vasodilation. This improved circulation can help to reduce the risk of blood clots, a common concern for individuals with heart conditions. Additionally, regular exercise contributes to lowering blood pressure by making the heart stronger and more efficient, thereby lessening the force needed to pump blood.

- **Reversing Heart Damage:**
  One of the most compelling aspects of exercise for those with CHF is its potential to reverse some of the damage to the heart. Research has shown that engaging in tailored exercise programs can lead to

improvements in the heart's structure and function. For example, exercise can promote the development of new blood vessels around blocked arteries, a process known as angiogenesis. This development can improve blood flow and oxygen delivery to the heart muscle, aiding in the repair of damaged tissues. While exercise is not a cure for CHF, it can be a powerful tool in mitigating the effects of heart damage and improving quality of life.

- **Overall Heart Function:**
  Regular physical activity has a beneficial effect on various factors that contribute to overall heart function. It can help reduce inflammation, a key component in the progression of heart disease. Exercise also aids in managing levels of cholesterol, reducing the buildup of plaque in arteries that can lead to further heart complications. Additionally, physical activity helps regulate blood sugar levels, decreasing the risk of developing diabetes, a condition that can significantly exacerbate CHF.

In conclusion, understanding the physiological benefits of exercise on the cardiovascular system reveals the undeniable value of incorporating regular physical activity into the management of CHF. By improving heart efficiency, enhancing circulation, potentially reversing heart damage, and supporting overall heart function, exercise can be a lifeline for those navigating the challenges of CHF. As with any significant lifestyle change, it's essential to consult with healthcare providers to tailor an exercise plan that is safe, effective, and aligned with individual health needs and goals. Embracing exercise as a vital component of CHF management can pave the way for a healthier heart and a more vibrant life.

Getting Started with Exercise: Navigating the Path to a More Active Life with CHF

Embarking on an exercise regimen when managing Congestive Heart Failure (CHF) can seem daunting at first. The fear of exacerbating your condition may loom large, overshadowing the known benefits of physical activity. However, with careful planning, clear communication with your healthcare team, and a personalized approach to exercise, you can safely begin a routine that supports your heart health and enhances your quality of life.

Discussing Your Exercise Plans with Healthcare Providers

- **Initiating the Conversation:**
  The first step in incorporating exercise into your CHF management plan is to have an open discussion with your healthcare provider. It's crucial to understand that not all exercises are suitable for everyone, and what works for one individual may not be safe or effective for another. Your healthcare team can assess your current health status, consider the severity of your CHF, and help determine the most appropriate types of physical activity for you.

- **Tailored Exercise Prescriptions:**
  During your discussion, emphasize the need for a tailored exercise prescription. A personalized plan takes into account your unique health challenges and goals, ensuring that the exercises recommended are both safe and beneficial. Your healthcare provider may suggest starting with low-intensity

102

activities, such as walking or water aerobics, gradually increasing intensity as your tolerance and fitness improve.

- **Interpreting Medical Advice into Actionable Plans:**
  Once you've received medical advice, the next step is to translate it into an actionable exercise plan. This means setting realistic goals, considering your current fitness level, and gradually increasing the duration and intensity of your workouts. Start with short sessions, maybe 10 to 15 minutes long, and slowly build up to longer periods as recommended by your healthcare team. It's also important to incorporate a variety of exercises to improve cardiovascular health, increase strength, and enhance flexibility, all while keeping your CHF management in mind.

Understanding Your Body's Signals

- **Monitoring Your Response to Exercise:**
  Listening to your body is paramount when exercising with CHF. Be alert to any new or worsening symptoms, such as unusual shortness of breath, chest pain, or excessive fatigue. If you experience any of these symptoms, stop exercising immediately and consult your healthcare provider. It's also beneficial to track your progress and any symptoms in a journal, which can be a useful tool for both you and your medical team to adjust your exercise plan as needed.

- **Adjusting Your Routine Based on Your Body's Feedback:**
  Your body's response to exercise will vary, and it's important to adjust your routine accordingly. Some days you may feel capable of more strenuous activity, while other days may require a more gentle approach. Flexibility in your exercise regimen is key to accommodating the fluctuations in your condition and ensuring that you remain within safe limits.

In conclusion, getting started with exercise when you have CHF requires careful consideration and planning, but it is an achievable and highly beneficial goal. By working closely with your healthcare providers to create a personalized exercise plan and paying close attention to your body's signals, you can safely incorporate physical activity into your life. This proactive approach can significantly contribute to managing CHF, improving your heart health, and enhancing your overall well-being.

Recommended Exercises for CHF Patients: A Path to Enhanced Heart Health

For those navigating life with Congestive Heart Failure (CHF), engaging in regular physical activity transcends the aim of merely enhancing heart function; it signifies a journey towards reclaiming quality of life. Tailored exercise programs serve as beacons of hope, empowering CHF patients by augmenting cardiovascular health, boosting endurance, and fortifying their bodies in a manner that is both safe and efficacious. This segment offers insight into four exercises particularly advantageous for CHF patients, laying the groundwork for a heart-health-conscious lifestyle.

Walking: A Gateway to Fitness

Walking is perhaps the most accessible form of exercise for CHF patients, serving as an excellent starting point for those new to exercise or returning after a hiatus. Its low-impact nature makes walking an ideal activity, minimizing stress on the heart while effectively boosting cardiovascular endurance. Regular walks, particularly at a brisk pace, can improve heart rate, strengthen the heart muscle, and increase stamina.

For CHF patients embarking on a walking regimen, the key is consistency and gradual progression. Start with short walks, aiming for 10 to 15 minutes daily, and gradually increase the duration as your fitness improves. Incorporate walking into your daily routine, whether it's a morning stroll, a walk after meals, or a leisurely walk with a friend. Remember, the goal is to build endurance without overexertion, so listen to your body and adjust your pace and duration accordingly.

Cycling: Low-Impact Cardiovascular Improvement

Cycling offers an effective cardiovascular workout with the added benefit of being low-impact, making it an excellent choice for CHF patients. Whether you opt for stationary cycling or outdoor biking, this activity helps to strengthen the heart and lungs, improve blood circulation, and build endurance—all crucial factors in managing CHF.

Start with moderate sessions, focusing on maintaining a steady, comfortable pace. As you gain strength and endurance, you can gradually increase the intensity and duration of your cycling workouts. For those preferring outdoor cycling, select flat, scenic routes that encourage consistency without the risk of overexertion.

Swimming: Full-Body Exercise for Heart Health

Swimming is a superb full-body workout that offers myriad benefits for CHF patients. The buoyancy of water reduces strain on the body, allowing for a comprehensive workout that strengthens the heart, tones muscles, and improves flexibility without putting undue stress on the joints.

Begin with gentle swimming techniques, focusing on controlled, smooth movements. Water aerobics or swimming laps can significantly enhance cardiovascular health, with the added advantage of being a refreshing, enjoyable activity. As with any exercise, it's crucial to start slowly, gradually increasing the intensity and duration of your swimming sessions as your body adapts.

Strength Training: Building Muscle to Support the Heart

Strength training is vital for CHF patients, helping to build muscle mass, which in turn supports heart function. By incorporating light weights, resistance bands, or bodyweight exercises into your routine, you can strengthen your muscles, improve metabolic health, and enhance overall physical resilience.

Begin with low-intensity exercises that target major muscle groups, prioritizing form and technique over weight or resistance. It's important to avoid heavy lifting, which can increase blood pressure and strain the heart. Instead, focus on exercises that allow for controlled, gradual strengthening of the muscles, such as seated leg presses, light dumbbell exercises, or resistance band workouts.

Incorporating walking, cycling, swimming, and strength training into your exercise regimen can provide comprehensive benefits for managing CHF. Each activity offers a unique set of advantages, from improving cardiovascular health to enhancing physical strength and flexibility. As always, consult with your healthcare provider before starting any new exercise program, ensuring that your chosen activities align with your health status and fitness goals. With the right approach, exercise can be a powerful ally in managing CHF, improving your heart health, and enhancing your overall quality of life.

Incorporating Exercise into Daily Routine: Sustainable Habits for Heart Health

For individuals managing Congestive Heart Failure (CHF), integrating exercise into the daily routine is pivotal, not just for immediate health benefits but for long-term well-being. The journey towards a heart-healthy lifestyle doesn't require drastic changes; rather, it's the small, consistent adjustments that can lead to significant improvements. This guide offers practical tips for seamlessly weaving exercise into your everyday life, ensuring sustainable habits that support your heart health.

Embrace Incremental Changes

The foundation of incorporating exercise into your daily routine lies in recognizing and utilizing the opportunities that your typical day presents. Small, incremental changes can collectively lead to considerable health benefits over time. One simple yet effective strategy is opting for the stairs rather than the elevator or escalator. This small decision not only strengthens your leg muscles but also gives your cardiovascular system a mini workout. Similarly, if you find yourself sitting for prolonged periods, set a timer to remind you to stand up and stretch or take a brief walk every hour. These micro-movements add up, contributing to your overall activity level without requiring a significant time commitment.

Discover Joy in Movement

Exercise doesn't have to be a chore or a routine task on your to-do list. Finding activities that you genuinely enjoy can transform exercise from a duty into a delight. Gardening, for example, offers a therapeutic and physically engaging pastime that not only beautifies your environment but also involves bending, lifting, and walking, all of which are beneficial for heart health. Similarly, dancing to your favorite music, whether alone or in a group setting, can be an exhilarating way to increase your heart rate while having fun. The key is to explore different activities until you find those that bring you joy and motivation to stay active.

Incorporate Walking into Your Routine

Walking is one of the most accessible forms of exercise, requiring no special equipment or environment. Look for opportunities to integrate walking into your day-to-day activities. For instance, consider walking to nearby destinations instead of driving, or park further away from the entrance of stores or your workplace to incorporate more steps into your day. If public transportation is part of your routine, getting off a stop early and walking the rest of the way can also increase your physical activity. Encourage family, friends, or colleagues to join you on walks, turning it into a social activity that benefits everyone involved.

Make Use of Technology

Technology can be a powerful ally in integrating exercise into your daily life. Various apps and devices are designed to monitor physical activity, set goals, and remind you to move. Utilizing these tools can provide a sense of progress and accomplishment, motivating you to stay active. Moreover, online exercise classes or video tutorials can offer guidance and variety, allowing you to explore new forms of exercise from the comfort of your home.

Create a Supportive Environment

Building a supportive environment is crucial for sustaining long-term exercise habits. Share your goals with friends and family, and encourage them to join you in your quest for a healthier lifestyle. Creating accountability and receiving support from loved ones can significantly enhance your motivation and commitment to daily physical activity.

Incorporating exercise into your daily routine is a journey of small steps leading to big rewards. By making manageable changes, seeking joy in movement, using technology to your advantage, and fostering a supportive environment, you can enhance your heart health and overall quality of life in the context of CHF management. Remember, the goal is to create sustainable habits that not only improve your physical health but also bring enjoyment and enrichment to your life.

Stress Management Techniques

Managing stress is paramount for individuals with Congestive Heart Failure (CHF), as stress can significantly impact heart health. This section explores the relationship between stress and heart health, introduces various stress management techniques suitable for individuals with CHF, and provides actionable advice for creating a lifestyle resistant to stress. By understanding and applying these techniques, individuals with CHF can better manage their condition, improve their quality of life, and potentially mitigate further heart complications.

The Connection Between Stress and Heart Health

Understanding the Impact

Stress is not just a psychological condition; it has profound physical implications, especially for the cardiovascular system. When we're stressed, our body's 'fight or flight' response is triggered, leading to a cascade of physiological reactions designed to help us face perceived threats. This response, while beneficial in short bursts, can have detrimental effects on heart health when sustained over long periods. For individuals with Congestive Heart Failure (CHF), the stakes are even higher.

- **Blood Pressure:** Stressful situations cause a temporary spike in blood pressure by increasing heart rate and narrowing blood vessels. Over time, repeated stress can lead to sustained high blood pressure, a major risk factor for heart damage and worsening CHF.

- **Irregular Heart Rhythms:** Stress can lead to arrhythmias—irregular heartbeats—that, while often benign, can be problematic for individuals with CHF, potentially exacerbating their condition.

- **Artery Damage:** Chronic stress is linked to inflammation, a key player in artery damage and the buildup of plaques. For those with CHF, managing stress is an integral part of preventing further heart damage and managing their condition effectively.

Physiological Effects

The body's response to stress is mediated by stress hormones like cortisol and adrenaline. These hormones prepare the body for immediate action but also exert effects on the cardiovascular system that can be harmful over time.

- **Cortisol:** Known as the 'stress hormone,' cortisol influences many functions within the body that are critical during stress reactions, including glucose metabolism, inflammatory responses, and blood pressure regulation. Prolonged exposure to high cortisol levels can lead to various cardiovascular issues, exacerbating CHF.

- **Adrenaline:** This hormone increases heart rate and blood pressure, preparing muscles for exertion. While this response is vital for survival, in modern life, where stressors are often not physical threats, it places unnecessary strain on the heart, particularly for those with existing heart conditions.

Long-Term Implications

The long-term implications of unmanaged stress on heart health cannot be overstated, particularly for individuals with CHF. Chronic stress not only exacerbates existing heart conditions but can also contribute to the development of new cardiovascular problems.

- **Worsening CHF Symptoms:** Continuous stress can lead to the worsening of CHF symptoms, including increased shortness of breath, swelling, and fatigue, due to the additional strain on the heart.

- **Heart Damage Reversal:** Managing stress effectively can help reverse some of the heart damage in individuals with CHF, improving overall heart function and enhancing quality of life.

- **Quality of Life**: Beyond physical health, effective stress management can significantly improve the quality of life for individuals with CHF, enabling them to engage more fully in daily activities and enjoy a better overall outlook on life.

Understanding the connection between stress and heart health is critical for individuals with CHF. By recognizing the impact of stress on the cardiovascular system, the physiological effects of stress hormones, and the long-term implications of chronic stress, individuals can appreciate the importance of effective stress management in managing their heart condition. The following sections will explore various stress management strategies to help individuals with CHF mitigate these risks and improve their heart health.

Stress Management Strategies

Creating an environment that minimizes stress and promotes heart health is vital, especially for those living with Congestive Heart Failure (CHF). Managing stress is not just about immediate relief; it's about building a lifestyle that supports long-term heart health. This section explores practical strategies and lifestyle changes that can help reduce stress and enhance the well-being of individuals with CHF.

1. **Deep Breathing Exercises**

   Deep breathing is a simple yet powerful tool for reducing stress. It can be performed anywhere, anytime, making it one of the most accessible stress management strategies. By focusing on slow, deep breaths, you can activate your body's relaxation response, counteracting the stress response and leading to immediate reductions in heart rate and blood pressure. Techniques such as the 4-7-8 method or diaphragmatic breathing can be especially beneficial. Practice deep breathing for a few minutes daily or whenever you feel stressed to help maintain calm and control.

2. **Meditation and Mindfulness**

   Meditation and mindfulness practices have been shown to significantly reduce stress levels, improve focus, and contribute to better heart health. By cultivating a state of mindfulness, you're training your mind to remain present and reducing the tendency to ruminate on past or future stressors. Guided meditations, mindfulness-based stress reduction (MBSR), and body scan techniques are all effective methods for achieving a meditative state. Regular practice can lower stress hormones, reduce inflammation, and improve overall heart function.

3. **Yoga**

   Yoga offers a unique combination of physical activity and mindfulness that can significantly benefit heart health. It helps reduce stress, lower blood pressure, and improve circulation and heart function. For individuals with CHF, gentle yoga poses and breathing exercises can be particularly therapeutic. Start with beginner-friendly poses and consider joining a class designed for those with heart conditions. Remember, the goal is not flexibility or strength but rather fostering a deeper connection between mind and body to reduce stress.

4. **Incorporating Routine**

   Consistency is key when it comes to stress management. Incorporating deep breathing exercises, meditation, and yoga into your daily or weekly routine ensures you reap ongoing benefits. Start small, perhaps with a morning meditation or yoga session, and gradually build these practices into your life. Setting specific times for these activities can help you maintain consistency.

Creating a Stress-Resistant Lifestyle

- **Adequate Sleep**

  Good sleep is foundational to managing stress and supporting heart health. Establish a relaxing bedtime routine, maintain a consistent sleep schedule, and create a sleep-conducive environment. Addressing sleep disturbances promptly and practicing good sleep hygiene can significantly improve the quality of your rest.

- **Social Support**

  A strong social network provides emotional support and can be a powerful stress reliever. Whether it's family, friends, or support groups, being connected with others can provide a sense of belonging and help you navigate the challenges of living with CHF.

- **Engaging in Hobbies**

  Hobbies and leisure activities offer an escape from daily stressors, providing joy and a sense of accomplishment. Whether it's gardening, painting, or any other hobby, find activities that relax and engage you.

- **Effective Time Management**

  Learning to manage your time effectively can significantly reduce stress. Prioritize your tasks, set realistic goals, and learn to delegate or say no when necessary. Balancing your commitments can help ensure you have time for the activities that support your heart health and well-being.

- **Diet and Exercise**

  A heart-healthy diet and regular physical activity play crucial roles in stress management and overall heart health. Refer back to previous sections for detailed guidance on incorporating exercise and nutritious foods into your lifestyle.

By adopting these stress management strategies and making them part of your routine, you can create a lifestyle that not only manages stress but also supports your heart health and improves your quality of life with CHF.

Bonus Chapter: 5 Special Occasions: Celebrating with Heart.

1. Walnut Crusted Salmon

Yield: 4 servings | **Prep time:** 15 minutes | **Cook time:** 20 minutes

Ingredients:

- 4 salmon fillets (6 ounces each)
- 1 cup walnuts, finely chopped
- 1 teaspoon garlic powder
- 1 teaspoon dried thyme
- 1/2 teaspoon salt
- 1/4 teaspoon black pepper
- 2 tablespoons olive oil
- Lemon wedges for serving

Directions:

1. Preheat the oven to 375°F (190°C). Line a baking sheet with parchment paper.

2. In a small bowl, mix together the chopped walnuts, garlic powder, dried thyme, salt, and pepper.

3. Brush each salmon fillet with olive oil, then press the walnut mixture onto the top of each fillet to form a crust.

4. Place the salmon fillets on the prepared baking sheet and bake for 15-20 minutes, or until the salmon is cooked through and the walnut crust is golden.

5. Serve the walnut crusted salmon with lemon wedges on the side.

Nutritional Information per serving:
310 calories, 34g protein, 3g carbohydrates, 18g total fat, 1g fiber, 0mg cholesterol, 85mg sodium, 800mg potassium, 1g sugars.

2. Heart-Healthy Paella

Yield: 4 servings | **Prep time:** 20 minutes | **Cook time:** 35 minutes

Ingredients:

- 1 cup brown rice
- 2 cups low-sodium vegetable broth
- 1/2 pound shrimp, peeled and deveined
- 1/2 pound chicken breast, cut into bite-size pieces
- 1 red bell pepper, sliced
- 1/2 cup frozen peas
- 1/2 cup diced tomatoes
- 2 cloves garlic, minced
- 1 teaspoon turmeric
- 1 teaspoon smoked paprika
- 1/2 teaspoon saffron threads (optional)
- 2 tablespoons olive oil
- Salt and pepper to taste
- Lemon wedges for serving

Directions:

1. In a large skillet or paella pan, heat the olive oil over medium heat. Add the garlic, red bell pepper, and chicken pieces. Cook until the chicken is browned on all sides.

2. Stir in the rice, smoked paprika, turmeric, and saffron threads. Cook for 2-3 minutes until the rice is well-coated in the spices.

3. Pour in the vegetable broth and bring to a simmer. Reduce the heat to low, cover, and cook for 20 minutes.

4. Add the shrimp, peas, and diced tomatoes. Cover and cook for an additional 10 minutes, or until the shrimp are pink and the rice is tender.

5. Adjust seasoning to taste. Serve with lemon wedges on the side.

Nutritional Information per serving:
270 calories, 18g protein, 40g carbohydrates, 6g total fat, 6g fiber, 0mg cholesterol, 200mg sodium, 500mg potassium, 4g sugars.

3. Heart-Healthy Herb-Roasted Turkey

Yield: 4 servings | **Prep time:** 15 minutes | **Cook time:** 120 minutes

Ingredients:

- 1 whole turkey (about 10-12 pounds), thawed
- 4 tablespoons olive oil
- 4 cloves garlic, minced
- 1 tablespoon fresh thyme, chopped
- 1 tablespoon fresh rosemary, chopped
- Salt and pepper to taste
- 1 lemon, halved (optional for added moisture and flavor)

Directions:

1. Preheat your oven to 325°F (165°C). Rinse the turkey and pat dry with paper towels. Remove any giblets from the cavity if present.

2. In a small bowl, mix together olive oil, garlic, thyme, and rosemary. Rub this mixture all over the turkey, under the skin, and inside the cavity. Season generously with salt and pepper.

3. If using, place lemon halves inside the turkey cavity. This will add moisture and a subtle citrus flavor to the meat.

4. Place the turkey breast-side up on a rack in a large roasting pan. Tent loosely with aluminum foil.

5. Roast in the preheated oven for about 2 hours, or until a meat thermometer inserted into the thickest part of the thigh reads 165°F (74°C). Remove the foil during the last 30 minutes of cooking to allow the skin to become golden and crispy.

6. Let the turkey rest for 20 minutes before carving. This allows the juices to redistribute, ensuring the meat is succulent.

Nutritional Information per serving:
220 calories, 40g protein, 0g carbohydrates, 5g total fat, 0g fiber, 0mg cholesterol, 70mg sodium, 330mg potassium, 1g sugars.

4. Celebration Citrus Salmon

Yield: 4 servings | **Prep time:** 10 minutes | **Cook time:** 20 minutes

Ingredients:

- 4 salmon fillets (about 6 ounces each)
- 2 tablespoons olive oil
- 1 orange, sliced
- 1 lemon, sliced
- 1 lime, sliced
- Salt and pepper to taste
- 1 tablespoon honey
- Fresh herbs (such as dill or parsley), for garnish

Directions:

1. Preheat your oven to 375°F (190°C). Line a baking sheet with parchment paper.

2. Arrange the salmon fillets on the baking sheet. Drizzle with olive oil and season with salt and pepper.

3. Top each salmon fillet with slices of orange, lemon, and lime.

4. Drizzle honey over the citrus-topped salmon.

5. Bake in the preheated oven for 15-20 minutes, or until the salmon flakes easily with a fork.

6. Garnish with fresh herbs before serving. Enjoy the harmonious blend of citrus flavors that make this dish a celebration on a plate.

Nutritional Information per serving:
260 calories, 34g protein, 8g carbohydrates, 8g total fat, 1g fiber, 0mg cholesterol, 85mg sodium, 650mg potassium, 3g sugars.

5. Heart's Delight Baked Cod with Herbs

Yield: 4 servings | **Prep time:** 15 minutes | **Cook time:** 20 minutes

Ingredients:

- 4 cod fillets (about 6 ounces each)
- 1 tablespoon olive oil
- 1 teaspoon dried basil
- 1 teaspoon dried oregano
- 1 teaspoon dried thyme
- 2 cloves garlic, minced
- Salt and pepper to taste
- 1 lemon, sliced
- Fresh parsley, for garnish

Directions:

1. Preheat your oven to 400°F (200°C). Grease a baking dish with a little olive oil.
2. Place the cod fillets in the prepared baking dish. Brush each fillet with olive oil.
3. In a small bowl, mix together the basil, oregano, thyme, and minced garlic. Sprinkle this herb mixture over the cod fillets. Season with salt and pepper.
4. Arrange lemon slices around the cod fillets in the dish.
5. Bake in the preheated oven for 18-20 minutes, or until the cod is flaky and cooked through.
6. Garnish with fresh parsley before serving. Enjoy a heart-healthy meal that's both delicious and nutritious.

Nutritional Information per serving:
200 calories, 40g protein, 3g carbohydrates, 2g total fat, 1g fiber, 0mg cholesterol, 80mg sodium, 470mg potassium, 0g sugars.

6. Majestic Mushroom & Barley Soup

Yield: 4 servings | **Prep time:** 15 minutes | **Cook time:** 40 minutes

Ingredients:

- 1 cup pearl barley
- 2 tablespoons olive oil
- 1 onion, finely chopped
- 2 garlic cloves, minced
- 1 pound mushrooms, sliced (mix of wild or button mushrooms)
- 4 cups low-sodium vegetable broth
- 2 cups water
- Salt and pepper to taste
- Fresh parsley, chopped for garnish

Directions:

1. Rinse the barley under cold water until the water runs clear. Drain and set aside.
2. In a large pot, heat the olive oil over medium heat. Add the onion and garlic, sautéing until softened, about 5 minutes.
3. Add the mushrooms and cook until they start to release their juices, about 8 minutes.
4. Stir in the barley, then add the vegetable broth and water. Bring to a boil, then reduce the heat to low, cover, and simmer until the barley is tender, about 30 minutes.
5. Season the soup with salt and pepper to taste. Serve hot, garnished with fresh parsley.

Nutritional Information per serving:
100 calories, 4g protein, 18g carbohydrates, 1g total fat, 4g fiber, 0mg cholesterol, 55mg sodium, 300mg potassium, 2g sugars.

7. Splendid Spinach & Feta Stuffed Chicken

Yield: 4 servings | **Prep time:** 20 minutes | **Cook time:** 25 minutes

Ingredients:

- 4 boneless, skinless chicken breasts
- 2 cups fresh spinach, chopped
- 1/2 cup feta cheese, crumbled
- 2 cloves garlic, minced
- 1 tablespoon olive oil
- Salt and pepper to taste
- Toothpicks or kitchen twine for securing

Directions:

1. Preheat the oven to 375°F (190°C). Lightly grease a baking dish with a bit of olive oil.

2. In a pan over medium heat, sauté spinach and garlic in olive oil until the spinach is wilted, about 3-5 minutes. Let cool slightly, then mix in the feta cheese.

3. Cut a pocket into the side of each chicken breast. Stuff the spinach and feta mixture into each pocket. Secure the pockets with toothpicks or kitchen twine.

4. Season the outside of the chicken breasts with salt and pepper. Place the stuffed chicken in the prepared baking dish.

5. Bake for 25-30 minutes, or until the chicken is thoroughly cooked and no longer pink in the center. Serve warm.

Nutritional Information per serving:
230 calories, 35g protein, 5g carbohydrates, 6g total fat, 2g fiber, 85mg cholesterol, 180mg sodium, 410mg potassium, 1g sugars.

8. Glorious Grilled Vegetable Platter

Yield: 4 servings | **Prep time:** 15 minutes | **Cook time:** 20 minutes

Ingredients:

- 1 zucchini, sliced into 1/4 inch rounds
- 1 yellow squash, sliced into 1/4 inch rounds
- 1 red bell pepper, seeded and cut into 1-inch pieces
- 1 yellow bell pepper, seeded and cut into 1-inch pieces
- 1 eggplant, sliced into 1/4 inch rounds
- 1 bunch asparagus, trimmed
- 2 tablespoons olive oil
- Salt and pepper to taste
- Optional: fresh herbs for garnish (such as parsley or thyme)

Directions:

1. Preheat your grill to medium-high heat.

2. Toss all the sliced and cut vegetables with olive oil in a large bowl. Season with salt and pepper to taste.

3. Arrange the vegetables on the grill (use a grill basket for smaller pieces if necessary) and cook for 10-15 minutes, turning occasionally, until the vegetables are tender and have grill marks.

4. Remove the vegetables from the grill and arrange them on a platter. Garnish with fresh herbs if desired.

5. Serve immediately as a healthy and colorful side dish.

Nutritional Information per serving:
140 calories, 4g protein, 18g carbohydrates, 7g total fat, 6g fiber, 75mg sodium, 520mg potassium, 8g sugars.

9. Radiant Raspberry & Almond Tart

Yield: 4 servings | **Prep time:** 20 minutes | **Cook time:** 25 minutes

Ingredients:

- 1 cup fresh raspberries
- 1/2 cup ground almonds
- 1/4 cup almond flour
- 2 tablespoons honey
- 1 egg, beaten
- 1/2 teaspoon vanilla extract
- Pinch of salt

Directions:

1. Preheat your oven to 350°F (175°C). In a mixing bowl, combine ground almonds, almond flour, and a pinch of salt.

2. Stir in the honey, beaten egg, and vanilla extract until a sticky dough forms.

3. Press the dough into a tart pan evenly. Prick the bottom with a fork.

4. Bake for 10 minutes, then remove from the oven.

5. Arrange fresh raspberries on the partially baked crust. Return to the oven and bake for an additional 15 minutes or until the edges are golden brown.

6. Let the tart cool before slicing. Serve and enjoy!

Nutritional Information per serving:
160 calories, 3g protein, 18g carbohydrates, 8g total fat, 3g fiber, 0mg cholesterol, 55mg sodium, 180mg potassium, 10g sugars.

10. Elegant Eggplant Rollatini

Yield: 4 servings | **Prep time:** 30 minutes | **Cook time:** 20 minutes

Ingredients:

- 2 large eggplants, sliced lengthwise into thin strips
- 1 cup ricotta cheese
- 1/2 cup grated Parmesan cheese
- 1 egg, lightly beaten
- 2 cups spinach, chopped
- 1 cup marinara sauce
- 1/2 cup shredded mozzarella cheese
- Salt and pepper to taste
- Fresh basil for garnish

Directions:

1. Preheat the oven to 375°F (190°C). Season eggplant slices with salt and let them sit for 10 minutes. Pat dry with paper towels.

2. Grill or roast eggplant slices until tender, about 5-7 minutes per side. Set aside to cool.

3. In a mixing bowl, combine ricotta, Parmesan, beaten egg, and spinach. Season with salt and pepper.

4. Spread a tablespoon of the cheese mixture on each eggplant slice, roll up tightly, and place seam side down in a baking dish.

5. Top eggplant rolls with marinara sauce and sprinkle with mozzarella cheese.

6. Bake in the preheated oven until the cheese is bubbly and golden brown, about 20 minutes.

7. Garnish with fresh basil before serving.

Nutritional Information per serving:
190 calories, 12g protein, 22g carbohydrates, 6g total fat, 7g fiber, 30mg cholesterol, 160mg sodium, 410mg potassium, 8g sugars.

As we turn the last page of "The Ultimate Congestive Heart Failure Cookbook" I hope your culinary journey has been as enlightening as it has been a pleasure for me to guide you. Born from a deep commitment to enhancing wellness through diet, this cookbook offers a roadmap for managing heart health with flavorful, heart-friendly meals. Navigating the challenges of heart health might seem overwhelming, yet I trust these recipes have brought ease, flavor, and healthful simplicity to your table.

Each recipe is more than a culinary formula; it is a beacon towards a healthier and more fulfilling lifestyle. The dietary choices you make hold the key to profound health transformations. Let these recipes serve not only as nourishment but also as daily companions on your path to longevity and wellness.

Continue to explore and adapt these recipes to your taste and health needs. Your diet is a critical element of your heart health toolkit—each meal a step towards a stronger heart.

If ever you need a spark of inspiration or face dietary hurdles, remember, you are part of a community committed to heart health. Engage with others, exchange experiences, and stay informed—the path to health is continually evolving.

Thank you for inviting this cookbook into your kitchen and heart health journey. May every dish you craft from these pages enrich your body and bring joy and accomplishment to your cooking endeavors.

To ongoing health and culinary discovery,

Sienna Currey

P.S. Stay tuned for future editions with more heart-healthy culinary creations. As your journey continues, so does our dedication to supporting you every step of the way.

Made in United States
North Haven, CT
05 October 2024